WE BELIEVE

Articles of Faith for the
Global Nazarene Family

WE BELIEVE

· · · · · · · · · · · · · · · · · · · ·

Articles of Faith for the
Global Nazarene Family

Frank Moore, Editor

CONTENTS

A WORD FROM THE EDITOR

by Frank Moore

God created a wonderful thing when he brought the Nazarene family together from around the world. Believers form this family from a wide variety of global areas, cultures, and language groups. Many social and cultural features differentiate Nazarenes from one another. We worship God in an array of styles. We all unite together, however, around the Articles of Faith. Regardless of our continents or native languages, Nazarenes share a common vocabulary when it comes to the Articles of Faith of the Church of the Nazarene.

At various times throughout our history, we have looked at the meaning and practical application of our Articles of Faith. This book follows in that tradition by offering a fresh review of our faith statements in the life of the faith community. The format of this review follows patterns of past books to a degree. However, this one has some important unique features. It offers a global perspective by listening to voices from every region of the Church of the Nazarene. It hears from an equal number of men and women. It gives careful attention to younger voices in the global church. And it illustrates that our Christian beliefs work in daily living whether you live in Memphis or Moscow, Buenos Aires or Bangkok. This book provides resources for personal enrichment and reflection as well as small group discussions.

It is essential that we get together often and discuss deeply the meaning and practical application of our Christian beliefs. Our world is currently floating in a sea of relativism that offers many options but few certainties. The internet brings millions of options for belief and living to our smartphones, tablets, and computers with the touch of a few keys. This endless array of possibilities often leaves readers confused and insecure. Many people feel unsure of their beliefs and conclude that they should remain open to a wide selection of options. This is a dangerous choice because we always end up living out in our daily actions what we believe in our heads and hearts. That is why it is so important to know what we believe and why we believe it.

Every time I think about the connection between belief and living, I am reminded of the tragic example of a biblical figure who misunderstood the character of God. He confused the way God interacts with his people. He misinterpreted godly preparation for successful leadership. Jephthah, one of the judges of Israel (Judges 10:6–11:40), offers a haunting biblical example of why we need to have correct beliefs about God and live in relationship with God so he can lead us. Scripture reminds us through the example of Jephthah: *we live in our actions what we believe in our hearts.*

Following a period of disobedience, the Hebrew people turned to God for deliverance from their enemies (Judges 10:15). They selected Jephthah to lead them in their fight against the Ammonites. God empowered Jephthah with his Spirit, guaranteeing victory. Perhaps Jephthah did not realize the Lord assured his victory; I don't know. But, on the way into battle, he bargained with God and vowed a foolish promise: "If you give the Ammonites into my hands, whatever comes out of the door of my house to meet me when I return in triumph from the Ammonites will be the LORD's, and I will sacrifice it as a burnt offering" (11:30–31).

The Spirit of God worked through Jephthah; they triumphed over the Ammonites in battle. Upon his return home, Jephthah's only child, his precious daughter, came out the door of his home first to greet her father. Verse 39 offers one of the most tragic lines in Scripture, "he did to her as he had vowed." Such deal-making to ensure victory commonly occurred in the pagan religions that surrounded the Hebrew people. These religions even promoted human sacrifices. Not true for our God. Yet, somehow, the beliefs of these other faiths crept into

Jephthah's thinking. His understanding of our God and his ways became misinformed. Tragically, he acted on those wrong beliefs and created a lifetime of heartache for his family. Remember, *we live in our actions what we believe in our hearts.*

Believers often say to me, "I really don't have any interest in reading about theology. I'm too busy to spend time learning our Christian beliefs." That's a dangerous perspective. Theology simply means "God talk;" every time we speak of our relationship with the Lord or our understanding of him, we communicate theology. Believers who have gone before us for the past two thousand years have read their Bibles and devoted their best thinking to give us a clearer picture of who God is and how he relates to his children. Their insights greatly enhance our Christian faith. What we believe about God and his purpose for our lives translates into our daily conduct.

I lived across the street from a man in my early years as a pastor. We became good friends. I urged him and his wife to attend our church, but they kindly refused my invitations. Why? Because my neighbor believed he had committed the unpardonable sin as a soldier fighting in World War II. Nothing I said ever persuaded him to accept God's forgiveness for his sins and become as a child of God. He resisted the invitation of God's Spirit because of his misguided belief about our faith.

I have dear friends who love God and desire to serve God. Yet they live in daily defeat because they believe they are hopelessly trapped in sin's grip as long as they possess a human body and live on this earth. A cycle of sinning and repentance haunts them daily. They can't claim the victory Paul proclaims in Romans 8:1–2: "Therefore, there is now no condemnation for those who are in Christ Jesus, because through Christ Jesus the law of the Spirit who gives life has set you free from the law of sin and death." They refuse to accept John's admonition: "My dear children, I write this to you so that you will not sin" (I John 2:1a).

The following chapters of this book offer information, stories, and illustrations both to encourage your faith and to clearly present beliefs of our Christian tradition as articulated in the Church of the Nazarene. We always want our God talk to be guided by the best thinking of the community of believers. Scripture, tradition, reason, and experience work together to shed light on our pathway. I urge you to give careful attention to your beliefs because *we live in our actions what we believe in our hearts.*

I trust the chapters of this book will enlighten your understanding of our beliefs and encourage you in your walk with Christ.

GOD THE ETERNAL, RELATIONAL CREATOR

by Kevin Mellish

Kevin Mellish is a professor of biblical studies at Olivet Nazarene University in Bourbonnais, Illinois.

I. The Triune God

1. We believe in one eternally existent, infinite God, Sovereign Creator and Sustainer of the universe; that he only is God, holy in nature, attributes, and purpose. The God who is holy love and light is triune in essential being, revealed as Father, Son, and Holy Spirit.

(Genesis 1; Leviticus 19:2; Deuteronomy 6:4–5; Isaiah 5:16; 6:1–7; 40:18–31; Matthew 3:16–17; 28:19–20; John 14:6–27; 1 Corinthians 8:6; 2 Corinthians 13:14; Galatians 4:4–6; Ephesians 2:13–18; 1 John 1:5; 4:8)

From the beginning, the Christian church has proclaimed its fundamental belief in the triune God. The theological doctrine of the Trinity states that God has appeared at various times in history as three distinct, independent persons—Father, Son, and Holy Spirit—while simultaneously existing as a single, unified being. For most of us (myself included), this notion defies logic and exceeds our ability to comprehend it. Although the fundamental elements of this doctrine have been carefully stated by church leaders, teachers, and theologians throughout history, the question of how the Trinity operates or functions in reality remains a divine mystery. It is with a sense of awe and wonder, then, that we recall the words of the famous hymn by Reginald Heber:

Holy, Holy, Holy, Lord God almighty
God in three persons, blessed Trinity

As we consider the topic of the triune God, we may wonder how it is possible for humans to understand what God is actually like. At its core, Christianity is a revealed faith. That is to say, all we know about God is what God imparts to us through revelation. Thankfully, God, through his abundant mercy and grace, has made himself known to humanity in various ways, such as creation.

The psalmist, for example, noted that, "The heavens are telling the glory of God; and the firmament proclaims his handiwork. Day to day pours forth speech, and night to night declares knowledge" (Psalm 19:1–2, NRSV).

In a similar way, the apostle Paul declared that, "God's eternal power and character cannot be seen. But from the beginning of creation, God has shown what these are like by all he has made" (Romans 1:20, CEV).

God has communicated information about God's character and being in other ways as well. God has shown us what he is like through events in history (such as the exodus or Pentecost); through God's word or instruction (see Psalm 19:7–11); and, ultimately, through the person of Jesus Christ (see John 1:1, 14). As a result of divine revelation, we can discover a lot about God.

God: The Eternal Being

From the time of the biblical writers until the present day, the people of God have repeatedly affirmed that God exists and that God is eternal in nature. These beliefs are clear from the opening statements of the Bible, which read, "In the beginning, God created . . ." (Genesis 1:1). The first words of Genesis indicate that God existed before time and creation began and that God's existence is not dependent upon the natural, material world.

Thus, God has no beginning or starting point—God just is. Because God's eternal existence was a fundamental belief for the biblical writers, atheism (the belief that God does not exist) was not an option. The psalmist forcefully asserted, "Fools say in their hearts, 'There is no God'" (Psalm 53:1a, NRSV).

Moreover, since God has no origins and exists independently of creation and time, God is also the creative source for all that has come into being. Furthermore, the church affirms the eternal nature of God. Just as God has no starting point or beginning, God also has no end. The biblical text highlights that God is "from everlasting to everlasting" (Psalms 41:13; 106:48, NRSV); that "he is the living God and the everlasting King" (Jeremiah 10:10, NRSV); and that he "shall not die" (Habakkuk 1:12, NRSV).

The various names for God in the Old Testament also indicate his eternal nature. God is called *El Olam*, meaning "the eternal or everlasting God" (Genesis 21:33, NIV and NRSV). God is also known by the name *Yahweh*. This name, which was revealed to Moses from the burning bush, is actually based on the Hebrew verb "to be," the very word for existence. Thus, the divine name *Yahweh* implies God's eternal being. When Moses wanted to know God's identity, God simply referred to himself as "I AM" (Exodus 3:14).[1]

God: The Creator of Heaven and Earth

The church also declares that the triune God is the Creator and Sustainer of this universe and all that is within it. Throughout the Old and New Testaments, the biblical writers affirm God's creative activity. The notion of God as Creator is so fundamental to God's identity that it literally permeates all portions of Scripture. References to God's role as Creator can be found, for example, in the Pentateuch (Genesis 1–3); the Prophets (Isaiah 40:12–28; Jonah 1:9); the Psalms (8; 74:12–17; 104); and the Wisdom Literature (Proverbs 8:22–30; Job 38–39).

In the New Testament, the apostle Paul reinforced this idea: "This God made the world and everything in it. He is Lord of heaven and earth, and he doesn't live in temples built by human hands. He doesn't need help from anyone. He gives life, breath, and everything else to all people" (Acts 17:24–25, CEV). The doctrine of God as Creator is

---

1. God also identifies himself in this verse as "I AM WHO I AM" or "I WILL BE WHAT I WILL BE."

integral to Christian theology and occupies a central role in the cardinal doctrines of the church.

The Nicene Creed, for instance, affirms this belief in its opening statement: "We believe in one God, the Father, the Almighty, maker of heaven and earth, of all that is, seen and unseen."[2]

As Creator, then, God rules as the sovereign Lord over everything he has brought into existence. All of creation belongs to him. Therefore, all creation is called upon to ascribe to the Lord praise and honor (Psalm 148:3–10). Since God created everything for his glory, honor, and purpose, all of creation finds its deepest fulfillment and meaning in its Maker.

God: The Relational Being

In addition to being eternal and Creator, God is also relational in nature. God desires a personal relationship with creation. Even though God is holy and transcendent, morally pure and righteous, perfect in wisdom and purpose, God covets fellowship with us humans beset by frailties, weaknesses, and disobedience. From the very beginning, God has shown his intentions to be intimately involved with us and with the world he brought into existence. In Genesis 2–3, for example, God created the man and woman, walked with them in the garden, and enjoyed regular communion with them.

God also entered into covenant relationships with his people at various times throughout history. In Hebrew, the word for "covenant" is *berith*. This term implies a binding or solemn agreement or oath made between two parties. It helped define the roles of the parties involved, thereby setting the parameters and guidelines for the relationship. God established this kind of relationship with Abraham, the father of the Israelite people (Genesis 15, 17), and with the people of Israel as well (Exodus 20–24).

God, in his mercy and grace, not only initiated covenant and called people into relationship with him, but he also provided the means by which the covenant relationship could be maintained. For the people of

---

2. Bruce L. Shelley, *Church History in Plain Language* (Nashville: Nelson, 1995), 102.

Israel, God provided instruction so they would know how to live in a way that was pleasing to him. God also commanded the people to construct the tabernacle, which symbolized the place where God's presence dwelled among the community and where offerings and sacrifices could be made (Exodus 26:30–37). Finally, God established the priesthood. The priests functioned as mediators, serving as the communicative link between God and the people of Israel as they represented the people before God and God before the people (Exodus 28–29; 39).

The metaphors that the Bible uses at times to describe God also imply God's intimate relationship with humanity. God is portrayed as a loving parent who taught his child to walk and as one who lifts an infant to his cheeks (Hosea 11:3–4). The Bible also refers to the people of Israel as God's son (Hosea 11:1). On other occasions, the intimacy between God and God's people is depicted as a marital relationship (Hosea 2). Familial language and metaphors extend into the New Testament, when the believer who is adopted as a child of God refers to God with the endearing term "*Abba*, Father" (Romans 8:15).

It is the relational nature of God, therefore, and God's intense desire to have fellowship with us that made it necessary for God to reveal himself later as a human being in the form of Jesus Christ and as spirit in the form of the Holy Spirit. By choosing to take on the form of human and spirit, God could relate to us in more personal and intimate ways.

Questions for Reflection or Discussion

Think about the material you have read in chapter 1 and consider your responses to the following questions. Use scriptural references to strengthen your answers whenever possible.

1. How old were you when you had your first awareness of God?

2. What promoted God's awareness to you?

3. What role does the world of nature play in giving you clues about God?

4. What role does the animal kingdom play in giving you clues about God?

5. What role does the beauty and mystery of outer space play in giving you clues about God?

6. What role do the intricacies and incredible complexity of our bodies play in giving you clues about God?

7. What role do the events in the natural world (weather patterns, seasons, etc.) play in giving you clues about God?

8. What role do the circumstances, cycles, and seasons of your life play in giving you clues about God?

9. What role does Jesus Christ play in informing you about God?

10. What role does the Bible play in informing you about God?

11. Considering the various aspects and sources named in questions 3–10, list as many attributes, characteristics, and qualities of God as you can.

12. Why does the Church of the Nazarene speak so often about God's attributes of holiness and love?

13. What does the Bible mean when it describes God as eternal?

14. What does the Bible mean when it says God has no origin and exists independently of creation and time?

15. What do you learn about God by studying the various names used in the Bible to identify God?

16. Why does God reveal God's self to us so clearly?

17. Compare God's desire for relationship with us to the loving relationship between parents and children.

18. How is our relationship with God like the relationship between a married couple?

19. Think about or discuss how we know and relate to God as Father, Son, and Holy Spirit.

20. Create an analogy or a diagram to explain the concept of the Trinity to a friend.

2 THE SAVIOR OF THE WORLD

by Filimao M. Chambo

Filimao M. Chambo serves as the director of the Africa Region of the Church of the Nazarene.

II. Jesus Christ

2. We believe in Jesus Christ, the second person of the triune Godhead; that he was eternally one with the Father; that he became incarnate by the Holy Spirit and was born of the Virgin Mary, so that two whole and perfect natures, that is to say the Godhead and manhood, are thus united in one person very God and very man, the God-man.

We believe that Jesus Christ died for our sins, and that he truly arose from the dead and took again his body, together with all things appertaining to the perfection of man's nature, wherewith he ascended into heaven and is there engaged in intercession for us.

(Matthew 1:20–25; 16:15–16; Luke 1:26–35; John 1:1–18; Acts 2:22–36; Romans 8:3, 32–34; Galatians 4:4–5; Philippians 2:5–11; Colossians 1:12–22; 1 Timothy 6:14–16; Hebrews 1:1–5; 7:22–28; 9:24–28; 1 John 1:1–3; 4:2–3, 15)

"An angel of the Lord appeared to him in a dream and said, 'Joseph son of David, do not be afraid to take Mary home as your wife, because what is conceived in her is from the Holy Spirit. She will give birth to a son, and you are to give him the name Jesus, because he will save his people from their sins'" (Matthew 1:20–21).

Jesus Christ is the second person of the triune Godhead. He was with God in the beginning, and through him all things were created

(John 1:2–3; Colossians 1:15–17). Through Jesus all things were created good, free from evil, and functioning as God intended (Genesis 1:4, 31). But when humankind chose evil over good, sin entered into the world and brought with it painful consequences. As a result of sin, the wickedness of the human race increased, and every inclination of the thoughts of human hearts became increasingly evil (Genesis 6:5).

The restoration of good in the creation of God now required redemption because we could not save ourselves from the mess we created. In God's wisdom and love, Jesus—through whom all things were created—was the Redeemer who came into the messy world that was created as good to bring restoration and salvation, to reconcile the world unto God.

His Miraculous Entrance

Marking the dawning of a new era was the miraculous, virgin birth of Jesus Christ. It was significant, something new, something that had never been seen before, and something that has not been seen since. Only God could perform this miraculous act. For the people of Israel, it was no secret that God's power and authority transcend the laws of nature. Isaac's birth (Genesis 21:1–7) and John the Baptist's (Luke 1) are examples of God's expression of his mighty works that transcend the laws of nature. However, the birth of Christ supersedes everything.

Jesus, "the image of the invisible God" (Colossians 1:15), the visible expression, true reflection, and physical representation of God, comes by the Holy Spirit and is born of the Virgin Mary so that two whole and perfect natures—the Godhead and humankind—are united in Jesus Christ, who is anointed and appointed by God to save the world. "The Holy Spirit will come on you, and the power of the Most High will overshadow you. So the holy one to be born will be called the Son of God" (Luke 1:35).

His Miraculous Ministry

Even though, throughout the Old Testament, the people of Israel anticipated the coming of the Messiah for their salvation, they seemed to have no expectation that he would come as he did. They also seem to have missed that God's plan for the restoration of the world would include Jesus's death on the cross and his resurrection on the third day. His birth, death, and resurrection are miraculous signs that find meaning in God. The miracles, signs, and wonders that Jesus performed are results of power that derives from the Father. The New Testament writers are in agreement that Jesus is from God and that God's power is at work in and through him as Jesus goes about the business of his Father to establish the kingdom of God—a kingdom that breaks into the world of darkness and actively works to reconcile the world to God.

Christ's death and resurrection further reveal God's image to the world. The expression of God's love for humanity and the possibility of forgiveness of sin, a transformed life, and a reconciled relationship with God in and through Christ (1 John 3:1–10) are for those who believe in Jesus Christ. And those who have been transformed by Christ are promised eternal life, which is made possible as a result of the victory of Christ over death (1 Corinthians 15:12, 20; 1 Thessalonians 4:13–18). The resurrection of Christ reassures us that God has power and authority over creation. Not even death can limit God's power. God can bring to life that which is dead. "Death has been swallowed up in victory" (1 Corinthians 15:54b).

His Miraculous Salvation

Therefore, even though the world is in a chaotic state and, because of sin and its consequences, things seem to be getting worse, there is great optimism for the healing of the human condition and the world. Through Jesus Christ, salvation is accessible for all! As people, communities, and villages call on the name of Jesus in repentance and receive the forgiveness of sin, all are empowered by the Lord to live victorious lives and to be witnesses of the new kingdom of God. Thus, Jesus commissions his followers, the church, to "go and make disciples of all nations, baptizing them in the name of the Father and of the Son and of the Holy Spirit, and teaching them to obey everything I have commanded you" (Matthew 28:19–20a).

The church, marked by Jesus Christ, must be the reflection and expression of Jesus Christ to the world. The church must derive its power from Jesus. Apart from Christ, we cannot and will not bear fruit (John 15:1–17). We are called to join in revealing Jesus to the world and to partner with Jesus in his mission to reverse the effects of sin. We are called to be the revelation of the breaking of the kingdom of God into the world of darkness. Those marked by Jesus become God's showcase to the world, witnessing to the fact that salvation and redemption are available to everyone. People do not have to live enslaved by the power of evil, for Christ has the power to set people free from evil and its power. Sin brought disorder into the world, but Christ's death provides a way to heal the world.

Jesus Christ not only sets us free from sin and its power, but he also sustains his creation. "In him all things hold together" (Colossians 1:17b). Thus, when we confess that we believe in Jesus Christ, we affirm that we put our trust in him and acknowledge that Jesus Christ's way of life is what God intends for all humanity. Believing in Jesus Christ means committing every aspect of our lives to his lordship. It is a choice to live in obedience to his teachings and in the assurance of hope that he sustains us with his mighty power.

Questions for Reflection or Discussion

Think about the material you have read in chapter 2 and consider your responses to the following questions. Use scriptural references to strengthen your answers whenever possible.

1. How does your understanding of Jesus expand when you consider that he was directly involved in the creation of our world (John 1:2–3; Colossians 1:15–17)?

2. Why is the virgin conception or birth of Jesus important to Christian faith?

3. Explain your understanding of how Jesus is 100% God and 100% man at the same time.

4. What do we learn about God's love for humanity when we realize God's plan of salvation for us included the death of Jesus on the cross?

5. What do we learn about God's power when we celebrate God raising the Son from the grave on the third day?

6. What is the reason for Christian believers' great optimism that God will heal the human condition and the world?

7. How does calling on the name of Jesus in repentance and receiving forgiveness for our sins change our lives?

8. How did Jesus's coming to our world usher the kingdom of God on earth in a new way?

9. Why did Jesus command his followers to "go and make disciples of all nations, baptizing them in the name of the Father and of the Son and of the Holy Spirit, and teaching them to obey everything I have commanded you" (Matthew 28:19–20a)?

10. What is your involvement in making disciples as Jesus commanded?

11. How might you improve in the endeavor to make disciples?

12. How are you and your community of faith reflections of Jesus Christ to your world?

13. How do we receive the divine power necessary to continue the work of Jesus Christ in our world?

14. Jesus has a mission to reverse the effects of sin in our world; how do we partner with him in that mission?

15. What evidence do you see that Jesus is involved in his mission to our world?

16. Sin enslaves people with addiction, bondage, regret, pain, and hopelessness; Jesus offers the power to set people free from sin. What are the best ways to get this message to those who need to hear it?

17. How does Jesus sustain our world as well as the personal lives of his followers?

18. What do we mean when we say Jesus is Lord?

3 LIFE IN THE SPIRIT
by Olivia Metcalf

Olivia Metcalf and her husband, Dustin, serve as directors of spiritual formation and as chaplains at Northwest Nazarene University in Nampa, Idaho.

III. The Holy Spirit

3. We believe in the Holy Spirit, the third person of the triune Godhead, that he is ever present and efficiently active in and with the church of Christ, convincing the world of sin, regenerating those who repent and believe, sanctifying believers, and guiding into all truth as it is in Jesus.

(John 7:39; 14:15–18, 26; 16:7–15; Acts 2:33; 15:8–9; Romans 8:1–27; Galatians 3:1–14; 4:6; Ephesians 3:14–21; I Thessalonians 4:7–8; 2 Thessalonians 2:13; I Peter 1:2; I John 3:24; 4:13)

I recently stood in Jessore, Bangladesh, in a hot, humid classroom in my bare feet, surrounded by students preparing for ministry. My husband, my parents, and I had been teaching a class on spiritual formation for the individual and the church. We had listened to the students' experiences and their testimonies. Since our time together was drawing to a close, we took Communion. Although we couldn't understand one another without an interpreter, there was a bond in that place, a community that was deep and broad. The Holy Spirit was there.

The Holy Spirit Has Always Been Here

In Genesis 1, the Spirit of God hovered over the waters, and creation came alive. In Genesis 2, God bent low and formed humans out of dust, and the breath (Spirit) of God brought them to life.

When God's people were enslaved in Egypt, he heard their cries for help. The story of Moses in the book of Exodus is about the Spirit coming upon an individual and enabling and empowering him to accomplish God's will in the world. The Hebrew people, dead in slavery, were brought to life as God's children by the Spirit's work.

Periods of exile, sin, despair, and separation in Scripture are marked by Spirit-filled prophets, who were used as voices of truth in a world of lies. Prophets always offer people the choice of death or life.

Then along came Jesus Christ, the Son of God. In his very first sermon, he read from the scroll of the prophet Isaiah and revealed that those ancient words were now being fulfilled. In Luke 4:18, Jesus said, "The Spirit of the Lord is on me." Jesus announced that his life, death, and resurrection would bring freedom, sight, hope, and life for all people. How would this take place? Jesus said it had to do with the Holy Spirit.

The early church, strengthened by the signs of the resurrection, met together in prayer and learning. In one of those gatherings the Spirit came and enabled them to do things they had never done before. Spreading the gospel is the important message of Acts 2—not the languages. When the Spirit comes upon us, there is new life.

The Holy Spirit Seems Hard to Pin Down

We *believe* that the Holy Spirit, one person of the Trinity, is moving and active in our world. But I think we struggle the most to *explain* the Spirit. Sometimes it is easier to understand God the Father, the Creator, the Source. We can wrap our minds around the Son of God, Jesus Christ, who had flesh and blood, joy and sorrow, temptation and victory, just as we do. The Spirit, however, is like the wind; I can feel it, but I can't see it. The Spirit is unpredictable and uncontrollable. The Holy Spirit is like tongues of fire.

Even though we believe in the Holy Spirit, we may not be able to define simply who the Spirit is. Scripture reminds us time and again that the Spirit is given and also gives. Maybe that's the place to begin. Our ancient fathers and mothers in the faith defined the Spirit as "the Lord, the Giver of life." That is the all-encompassing definition. The Holy Spirit gives wholeness of life.

25

We believe that this giving of life begins with conviction, which is not a very pleasant gift, really. What we do with the conviction we all experience is crucial. If we see the convicting gift of the Spirit as a curse, then we won't receive the further gifts of the Spirit. We must listen to the Spirit and repent of our sins because this is how the Spirit is able to give us life.

When we receive this life, we would do well to remember that the Holy Spirit is the one who does the convicting. Christians too often take this work into their own hands, and much damage is done. We are called to be light and salt, not judge and jury. When we live in Christ, by the Spirit, we are salt and light. We season and bring light to the world in such a way that the convicting work of the Spirit can be experienced because of the contrast we provide. The Spirit convicts. We are called to live faithfully.

After conviction and repentance comes the gift of regeneration. This is the experience of salvation. It is new life. Jesus Christ, through his life, death, and resurrection, has made a way for us be in a right relationship with God. We were dead in our sins; now we are alive in Christ through the Spirit. This life comes with a responsibility. We are not called to condemn; rather, we are called to be vessels of life!

The Holy Spirit Brings Divine Partnership

The gift we receive from the Spirit isn't meant to be saved for some future use. Life in the Spirit is meant to be shared right now. We are invited to partner with God to bring life. Where there are brokenness and despair, we can offer people healing and hope through the Spirit. Where there are loss and confusion, we can bring meaning and truth through the Spirit.

Sanctification is the gift that follows regeneration. We cannot earn sanctification. We cannot do enough good deeds to deserve holiness. We cannot go through exactly the right motions, go to enough church services, or memorize enough Scripture to tally up points for sanctification. The Spirit gives us this wholeness of life. As we grow, as we surrender, as we learn to love God and others, by God's grace we are prepared to receive sanctification. When we develop in our relationship with God, we will be ready to experience the fullness the Spirit gives—the gift of perfect love for God and others.

The Holy Spirit's Work Never Ends

Risk enters the equation when we allow ourselves to believe that sanctification is the end of the Spirit's work. We might believe we have arrived and have nothing more to receive from the Spirit. Yet there is a further gift to receive, and that is growth. Without growth, there is no life. We are to continue to learn, to know, and to experience the person of Christ. The Spirit enables growth.

If we are open and willing to be taught, there is no end to the work of the Spirit in us. We must be people who study God's Word, worship with other believers in unity, keep our eyes focused on Jesus, and receive the work of the Spirit daily.

The signs of our lives, shaped by the Spirit's work, will be fruit. "But the fruit of the Spirit is love, joy, peace, forbearance, kindness, goodness, faithfulness, gentleness and self-control. Against such things there is no law" (Galatians 5:22–23). People often speak of the fruit of the Spirit as miracles. I have even heard people say that, unless there are miraculous deeds done, the Spirit is not present. Let us remember that the fruit of a Spirit-filled life is miraculous in and of itself.

The world needs to see Christ followers who love, lead joyful lives, and make peace in a violence-filled world. The world is desperate for Christians who are patient, kind, good, and faithful. People long for Christian witnesses who are gentle and have self-control in the out-of-control sinfulness around us. If we could exhibit these gifts of the Spirit, our marriages, families, friendships, workplaces, schools, communities—in fact, the whole world—would be different because of the life-giving work of the Spirit in us.

I am grateful to be part of something bigger than myself. The world tells me that I am meant to desire wealth, power, and safety. I could believe this if I didn't know better. Thankfully, the church has taught me that I am made in the image of God; I am meant to be made whole, growing in the likeness of Christ by the work of the Holy Spirit. That day in Bangladesh, I felt the camaraderie of brothers and sisters experiencing the power of the Holy Spirit, being shaped and formed into the image of Christ, and bringing life to the world through the transformative work of the Spirit.

Whenever order comes from chaos, the Spirit is at work.

Whenever hope springs up from despair, the Spirit is at work.

Wherever there is life, the Spirit is at work.

May our desire be now, and always, to keep in step with the Holy Spirit (Galatians 5:25).

Questions for Reflection or Discussion

Think about the material you have read in chapter 3 and consider your responses to the following questions. Use scriptural references to strengthen your answers whenever possible.

1. How would you explain the person of the Holy Spirit to someone wanting to learn more about the Christian faith?

2. How would you explain the work of the Holy Spirit to someone wanting to learn more about the Christian faith?

3. Why do many people find it more difficult to describe the Holy Spirit than the Father and the Son?

4. Acts 2 tells the story of the coming of the Holy Spirit in new ways at Pentecost. His coming resulted in Christ's followers sharing the gospel message with everyone who would listen. How does the Holy Spirit work in us to share the gospel message today?

5. Give examples of the Holy Spirit convicting individuals of their sin.

6. How is our repentance of sin a gift from God?

7. How does the Holy Spirit use our repentance of sin and expressions of faith in Jesus to bring new life (regeneration)?

8. What does the author of this chapter mean when she says, "We are called to be light and salt, not judge and jury"?

9. How do we partner with God to offer new life to those who need it?

10. What is the gift of the Spirit that the Bible calls sanctification?

11. How does God's gift of sanctification fill us with perfect love for God and others?

12. How do you explain the progressive growth that happens in believers' lives as they continue to learn, know, and experience the person of Christ?

13. How does the Spirit teach us as we:
    - Study God's Word?
    - Worship with other believers in unity?
    - Keep our eyes focused on Jesus?
    - Receive the work of the Spirit daily?

14. Describe how the fruit of the Spirit listed in Galatians 5:22–23 manifest themselves in believers' lives.

15. How do we manifest God's power at work in the world as we live daily lives that manifest the fruit of the Spirit?

16. How does the Spirit grow us in the likeness of Christ as we follow him daily?

17. Give examples of the Holy Spirit at work:
    - Bringing order from chaos?
    - Giving hope in times of despair?
    - Offering life?

THE MEANING OF LIFE
by Jorge L. Julca

Jorge L. Julca is rector of Seminario Teológico Nazareno del Cono Sur in Buenos Aires, Argentina, and the regional education coordinator for the South America Region.

IV. The Holy Scriptures

4. We believe in the plenary inspiration of the Holy Scriptures, by which we understand the sixty-six books of the Old and New Testaments, given by divine inspiration, inerrantly revealing the will of God concerning us in all things necessary to our salvation, so that whatever is not contained therein is not to be enjoined as an Article of Faith.

(Luke 24:44–47; John 10:35; 1 Corinthians 15:3–4; 2 Timothy 3:15–17; 1 Peter 1:10–12; 2 Peter 1:20–21)

Editor's note: Out of God's love for creation comes a desire to communicate with us. Over time, verbal accounts of God's interaction with humanity led to written versions of these stories. The written Word grew as alphabets, writing instruments, and additional methods of nonverbal communication came into existence.

As the Church of the Nazarene, we have created our theological and doctrinal journey throughout the history of the church. All along that road, Scripture has been paramount in the life of our church. Scripture has not only been part of our reformed inheritance from the sixteenth century (*sola Scriptura*), but it has also constituted our Arminian and Wesleyan legacy. Jacobus Arminius wrote, "Only in Scripture we have the infallible word of God, and nowhere else."

Hope of Redemption

Scripture tells us about the history of salvation, which extends from Genesis to Revelation. It offers us God's self-revelation through his mighty acts as well as through the Word made flesh, his Son, Jesus Christ. God's main purpose throughout Scripture is to offer humanity the hope of redemption from sin and death. Along with that purpose, there is perfect harmony between the prophets, the words of Jesus, and the apostles around the Bible's essential message.

Our identity and belonging as Nazarenes can be broken down into a few, fundamental aspects. One has to do with our acceptance of the plenary inspiration of the sixty-six books that make up the Old and New Testaments. Plenary inspiration means that the Bible in its entirety is the Word of God. This belief implies our acknowledgment that all biblical authors, belonging to various social strata, wrote in different literary genres from within their own contexts, cultures, and backgrounds. But we also acknowledge that all Scripture was inspired by the Spirit (2 Timothy 3:16). The Bible represents a marvelous integration of diversity and unity with a redeeming purpose.

The Nazarene interpretation about the inspiration of Scripture also holds in correct balance the divine-human element of the Scripture and shares the same dual nature of the Word made flesh. This christological analogy gives evidence of another distinctive aspect of the declaration of faith that Scripture "inerrantly reveal[s] the will of God concerning us in all things necessary to our salvation." Understanding this is of utmost importance. Here lies the recognition that, in this dynamic process, God, through the Holy Spirit, ensured the existence of an accurate and truthful record of his will, including all things pertinent to our redemption in Christ.

What to Believe and How to Live

Scripture's relevance in the Christian faith as the standard of faith and conduct proves fundamental. Through Scripture we know God, who reveals himself to establish what we should believe (our doctrine, our declaration of faith), including the way in which we should live (our code of ethics).

However, perhaps the most repeated questions relating to the Bible and its message have to do with its applicability and relevance to everyday life. We might ask ourselves: What good is the Bible? In spite of the historical gap that separates us from the time when it was written, does the Word have answers for us today? Can we trust its message?

The author of Hebrews left us a clear and simple declaration: "For the word of God is alive and active. Sharper than any double-edged sword, it penetrates even to dividing soul and spirit, joints and marrow; it judges the thoughts and attitudes of the heart" (4:12). The first affirmation highlights the Bible's validity, its faithfulness, and its relevance to our present situations. It means that Scripture has no expiration date and will never be a thing of the past. It is more current than tomorrow's newspaper. As a result, we can trust it. No less important is the second affirmation about Scripture's efficiency. According to Hebrews 4:12, we can be confident that the Word gives results, has power, offers relief and direction, and transforms lives.

Meaning of Life

The Word of God is not a science book, nor is it a history book. It was not written to dissipate human curiosity. Instead, it has the answers to all human beings' existential questions pertaining to the meaning of life. This means that, beyond just reading Scripture, it is imperative that we obey it daily. John Wesley said, "The Spirit of God not only once inspired those who wrote [the Bible], but continually inspires, supernaturally assists, those that read it with earnest prayer."[1]

Throughout the Old and New Testaments, references to the benefits of obeying the Word of God abound:

Those who delight in it reap a solid, firm, and growing life (Psalm 1).

The person who obeys its commandments brings light to his or her path (Psalm 119:105).

The one who is led by divine counsel finds the right path to reach the purpose for which he or she was created (Psalm 119:121–135).

---

1. John Wesley, *Explanatory Notes upon the New Testament* (London: Epworth Press, 1941), 794.

Those who abide by its teachings find the way out of temptation (Matthew 4:1–11).

Individuals who keep the Word live in communion with God (John 14:15–23).

Proverbs 4:20–22 is a clear invitation to listen, read, obey, and keep the Word of God at the center of a victorious Christian life: "My son, pay attention to what I say; turn your ear to my words. Do not let them out of your sight, keep them within your heart; for they are life to those who find them and health to one's whole body."

The verbs used in these verses refer to our relationship with the Word. They show an increasing intensity, and the invitation turns into a command. Keeping the Bible close leads to the immediate results of finding meaning for our lives as well as healing from all kinds of ailments, both spiritual and physical.

All through the history of humanity, millions of people have been inspired by the moral and ethical teachings of holy Scripture. Many have been redeemed by its message. As they obeyed its precepts, they discovered the secret to a full and abundant life as intended by our Creator.

Guide for Community of Faith

Finally, we also need to acknowledge that the influence of the Word of God transcends the individual realm and reaches the sphere of the community of faith. From this perspective, we must ask ourselves: What place does the Word occupy in our work as the church today? In what measure do our models of worship and liturgy, preaching, leadership, or pastoring pass through the filter of the Word and are molded by it?

As we travel along new roads as a denomination, holding steady to our inheritance in relation to the centrality of Scripture will help us to remain in the counsel of God. This perspective helps us find pertinent and biblically sound answers as we face the new challenges of our generation.

Questions for Reflection or Discussion

Think about the material you have read in chapter 4 and consider your responses to the following questions. Use scriptural references to strengthen your answers whenever possible.

1. What does the author of this chapter mean when he says, "Scripture has no expiration date and will never be a thing of the past?"

2. The concept of *sola Scriptura* comes from the Latin phrase meaning "Scripture alone," which means that Scripture is the ultimate source of direction for faith and practice. Why is this concept so important to the Church of the Nazarene?

3. How does Scripture unfold God's history of salvation for humanity?

4. How does God reveal who God is and how God works in the pages of Scripture?

5. Give examples from Scripture of God's mission of offering us the hope of redemption from sin and death.

6. What do Nazarenes mean when they talk about the "plenary inspiration" of Scripture?

7. Identify examples of divine and human elements in Scripture.

8. Nazarenes believe that the Bible reveals God's will with regard to everything necessary for our redemption in Christ. How does this understanding differ from those who believe the Bible is a source of authority on all subjects, such as science and history?

9. Give examples of how the Bible reveals God's will on:
   • What we should believe?
   • How we should live?

10. How does the Bible speak to our everyday issues of living?

11. What is the relationship between the Holy Spirit and the Bible?

12. What gives the Bible the ability to:
    • Bring results in people's lives when they read it?
    • Offer relief and direction?
    • Transform lives?

13. Give examples of the Bible answering a central question of human existence: What is the meaning of life?

14. How does the Holy Spirit continually inspire and supernaturally assist those who read the Bible with earnest prayer?

15. Name some of the practical benefits of obeying the Word of God.

16. How does the Bible reveal the secret to the full and abundant life intended by God?

17. In what ways does the Bible offer direction for worship, preaching, leadership, and pastoring in the community of faith?

18. What essential role does the Bible play in your life?

5 FREEDOM FROM SIN

by Svetlana Khobnya

Svetlana Khobnya is a lecturer in biblical studies at Nazarene Theological College in Manchester, England.

V. Sin, Original and Personal

5. We believe that sin came into the world through the disobedience of our first parents, and death by sin. We believe that sin is of two kinds: original sin, or depravity, and actual or personal sin.

5.1. We believe that original sin, or depravity, is that corruption of the nature of all the offspring of Adam by reason of which everyone is very far gone from original righteousness or the pure state of our first parents at the time of their creation, is averse to God, is without spiritual life, and inclined to evil, and that continually. We further believe that original sin continues to exist with the new life of the regenerate, until the heart is fully cleansed by the baptism with the Holy Spirit.

5.2. We believe that original sin differs from actual sin in that it constitutes an inherited propensity to actual sin for which no one is accountable until its divinely provided remedy is neglected or rejected.

5.3. We believe that actual or personal sin is a voluntary violation of a known law of God by a morally responsible person. It is therefore not to be confused with involuntary and inescapable shortcomings, infirmities, faults, mistakes, failures, or other deviations from a standard of perfect conduct that are the residual effects of the fall. However, such innocent effects do not include attitudes or responses contrary to the spirit of Christ, which may properly be called sins of the spirit. We believe that personal sin is

primarily and essentially a violation of the law of love; and that in relation to Christ sin may be defined as unbelief.

(Genesis 3; 6:5; Job 15:14; Psalm 51:5; Jeremiah 17:9–10; Matthew 22:36–40; Mark 7:21–23; John 8:34–36; 16:8–9; Romans 1:18–25; 3:23; 5:12–14; 6:15–23; 7:1–8:9; 8:18–24; 14:23; 1 Corinthians 3:1–4; Galatians 5:16–25; 1 John 1:7–2:4; 3:4, 7–10)

Nobody has to teach us to give preference to ourselves and our desires. We come into this world with self clearly in first place. Children on the playground illustrate this phenomenon well. Original sin speaks to the sinful human condition. William Greathouse, former general superintendent, scholar, and theologian in the Church of the Nazarene, explained this condition by comparing it to a disease.[1] This disease is a moral and spiritual depravation. The human heart is crooked toward self and inevitably disobeys God. We do not say an individual is guilty before God due to original sin. This type of sin can only tempt us to disobey God and prefer our way to his ways. However, when we yield to temptation, we become responsible for personal sin. Sin as a disease, nevertheless, is fatal if not treated.

Although the language of a disease is helpful, we need to say more. There are genetic and hereditary diseases. Those who have them are innocent victims with some sort of incurable deficiency. Other diseases can be cured and no longer affect individuals. Some diseases just go away on their own, and nothing needs to be done about them. But sin differs from all of these. Perhaps some further light can come with another look at Scripture.

Broken Relationship with God

In the biblical story, human history begins without sin. Sin only enters the picture as the consequence of breaking away from God's grace in Genesis 3. So sinfulness was not the natural state of humanity. Humanity was created to live in ongoing relationship with God the Creator. Naturally, we needed God, and he never stopped searching to

---

1. William Greathouse, "Article 5: Sin, Original and Personal," *Holiness Today* (March 2004), 16–17.

restore the relationship with us. We observe this truth in God calling Adam and his descendants; in Abraham's covenantal relationship with God; and, ultimately, in reconciliation through Christ. Sin, therefore, is primarily relational. Both Genesis and Romans depict the sinful human condition as alienation from a relationship with God. It starts as a marred relationship with God but leads to even greater iniquity and has greater consequences (Romans 6:23).

The Bible draws a picture of sin on a global scale as an uncontrolled power that affects the whole universe. It makes its way through the human rebellion to the world, enslaving everyone. As people yield to their temptations, minds and intentions become clouded. Sin affects and twists our humanity so that we inevitably become sinners. God's law, God's people, and the whole creation all become diverted from God's original intentions. Spiritual death and the fear of physical death result. Sin becomes a slave master, resulting in total bondage from which people cannot free themselves (Romans 6:16, 20).

On the one hand, sin becomes personal. It is our self-centered direction away from God. The Bible is clear in stating that: "All have sinned" (Romans 3:23). Death came through sin, but it spread to all because all have sinned (Romans 5:12). No one escapes the power of sin (Psalm 51). Paul speaks of our solidarity in Adam (Romans 5:12). In a way, each of us reenacts the fall, and we are personally responsible for our sinful actions (Ezekiel 18; 1 John 3:4).

On the other hand, sin also has all-encompassing and corporate consequences. When the relationship with God is distorted, all relationships become twisted, and all the spheres of life are affected. Sin corrupts the human race—not only individuals, but also families, societies, politics, economics, and culture.[2] All people share solidarity in their accumulated sinfulness because we all are members of one another and affect one another. We all are born into an environment where sin is already present and where it is easier to do evil than to be guided by

---

2. T. A. Noble, *Original Sin and the Fall: Definitions and a Proposal in Darwin, Creation and the Fall*, ed. R. J. Berry and T. A. Noble (Nottingham: Apollos [an imprint of InterVarsity Press], 2009), 126.

good. Creation also shares in the consequences of the sinful human condition and groans in anticipation of its redemption from its current futility (Romans 8:19–20).

Sin's Cure

So, what is sin's cure? What brings freedom? What is the biblical view on the solution to the problem of sin?

As a disease, sin requires intervention. The cure involves God's forgiving and healing grace and our commitment to Christ's restoration. To release us from the power of sin and the spirit of slavery, Christ took on our human condition and defeated sin by his obedient life and death on the cross (Hebrews 4:15). Christ came into solidarity with humanity, yet he remained faithful and obedient in relationship with the Father so that in Christ we may be restored. We may participate in a new solidarity with Christ and his obedience. Through him, we may remain in the divine domain and be equipped to resist sin.

Sin Pardoned, Relationship Restored

Since sin affects all of us personally, we all need to be crucified with Christ in order to be pardoned and restored in our relationship to God (Galatians 2:19–20). Moreover, since we still live in the fallen world, we continuously need to learn Christ (Ephesians 4:20–24) and be guided by his Spirit (Galatians 5:22–25).

The solution to sin is based on corporate salvation in Christ. Paul, in particular, argues that corporate solidarity in the obedience of Christ is much more than a match for the corporate solidarity that flows from Adam (Romans 5:17–21).[3] God's inconceivable offer in Christ is to reconcile all to himself. God in Christ wants to deliver humanity from sin in all its aspects, including personal, social, political, economic, and environmental. The communal language sets the stage for those in Christ to have corporate influence among themselves (as the body of Christ) and in the world. Those in Christ are corporately engaged and may influence

---

3. Kent E. Brower, "The Human Condition in Romans," *European Explorations in Christian Holiness*, vol 2 (Manchester: NTC, 2001), 227.

one another, their societies, and the rest of the world in the loving and transformative ways of Christ until the final conquest of sin at Christ's coming again.

That conquest presumes dying and rising with Christ (Romans 6:11). Dying to sin and rising with Christ is a powerful concept that invites us to empty ourselves and let the Holy Spirit fill us completely. In Christ, sin will not be our master (Romans 6:14). With our mind set on Christ and filled with the Spirit of Christ (Romans 8:10), we need ongoing transformation. Having committed ourselves to God in Christ by the Spirit, we must continue to resist the power of evil in the world (Ephesians 6:10–18). We need Christ and his Spirit living and reigning within us through and through!

Questions for Reflection or Discussion

Think about the material you have read in chapter 5 and consider your responses to the following questions. Use scriptural references to strengthen your answers whenever possible.

1. Give examples of the ways original sin directs everyone, including children, to give preference to themselves and their own personal desires.

2. How is sin like a disease?

3. How does sin differ from a disease?

4. Why is the temptation to sin so powerful?

5. Why did God never stop searching for lost humanity after humanity sinned?

6. In what ways are all sins an alienation from relationship with God?

7. How is sin a power that affects the entire world?

8. Give examples of how sin becomes a slave master, bringing total bondage from which people cannot free themselves.

9. How does sin bring spiritual death and hasten physical death?

10. How do the consequences of personal sins affect families, societies, politics, economics, and culture?

11. Naturally speaking, why is it easier to do what we want to do than to be guided by God's good purposes for us?

12. What is the cure for sin?

13. How did Christ Jesus make it possible for us to be freed from the power and dominion of sin?

14. How does Christ bring to believers deliverance from sin that is personal, social, political, economic, and environmental?

15. How does Christ's redemption from sin operate within the community of faith and the body of believers?

16. Explain in simple terms how believers die to sin and are raised to new life in Christ.

17. How does the Holy Spirit transform the lives of Christ followers?

18. How does the Holy Spirit assist Christ's followers in resisting temptation?

19. Why do we call our redemption new life in Christ?

20. What is your testimony regarding Christ's deliverance from sin in your life?

6 TO BE AT ONE

by Thomas A. Noble

Thomas A. Noble is a professor of theology at Nazarene Theological Seminary in Kansas City and a visiting lecturer and PhD research supervisor at Nazarene Theological College in Manchester.

VI. Atonement

6. We believe that Jesus Christ, by his sufferings, by the shedding of his own blood, and by his death on the cross, made a full atonement for all human sin, and that this atonement is the only ground of salvation, and that it is sufficient for every individual of Adam's race. The atonement is graciously efficacious for the salvation of those incapable of moral responsibility and for the children in innocency but is efficacious for the salvation of those who reach the age of responsibility only when they repent and believe.

(Isaiah 53:5–6, 11; Mark 10:45; Luke 24:46–48; John 1:29; 3:14–17; Acts 4:10–12; Romans 3:21–26; 4:17–25; 5:6–21; 1 Corinthians 6:20; 2 Corinthians 5:14–21; Galatians 1:3–4; 3:13–14; Colossians 1:19–23; 1 Timothy 2:3–6; Titus 2:11–14; Hebrews 2:9; 9:11–14; 13:12; 1 Peter 1:18–21; 2:19–25; 1 John 2:1–2)

There are many aspects to our faith, but everything is centered on the gospel of "Christ crucified" (1 Corinthians 1:23; Galatians 3:1). We need to address five important phrases in this Article of Faith.

Jesus Christ

First, everything hinges on our Lord Jesus Christ. In Article II, we have already said that we believe in Jesus Christ. That's important! It is not just that we believe things *about* him. We believe that he died for our sins (1 Corinthians 15:3). We believe in him. We trust him. It's a personal relationship. We trust him so much because we know he died to save us. He loved us enough to suffer for us. But the key to this is grasping *who* died. God incarnate suffered for us. God incarnate gave himself up to an agonizing death on the cross—and that is the measure of his love.

A Full Atonement

The English word *atonement* was first coined by the Bible translator William Tyndale as "at-one-ment"—to make two who are opposed to be "at one." That is to say, atonement means reconciliation. So somehow the death of Christ on the cross reconciled us to God.

But the English word *atonement* has a second meaning. The verb *to atone* was used in the English Bible to translate a Hebrew verb, *kpr* (transliterated "kaphar" and pronounced "kaw-far"), which is used for the Old Testament sacrifices. Some of the sacrifices atoned for Israel's sin, particularly those on the annual Yom Kippur, the Day of Atonement. This context gives us a clue about how the death of Christ reconciled us to God.

Athanasius, bishop of Alexandria in the fourth century AD and one of the greatest theologians of the ancient church, explained in his book *On the Incarnation* that God faced a dilemma. (Obviously, this is a very human way to speak of God, but it helps us understand the mystery.) The dilemma was that he passionately loved the human creatures he had created but that they had disobeyed and rebelled against him. Consequently they were destroying themselves. But God couldn't say, "Oh, it doesn't matter." It did matter. To flout God's holy love would be to destroy God's good creation. The law that gave the universe order had to be kept. Therefore, God took on the consequences by becoming our representative in Jesus, the new head of the human race. He offered his body, writes Athanasius, "as a substitute for all, fulfilling the debt by his death."

So God the Son, as a human being, offered himself as the ultimate sacrifice in order to satisfy not just God's justice and wrath but also his own love. Jesus, the new head of the race, embodying humanity, offered to God what only he could offer—the most ultimate possible offering of loving, self-sacrificing obedience. Love responded to love. God and humanity are therefore at one again through the cross.

The Only Ground of Salvation

According to Paul, we need to be saved from sin, from death, from the principalities and powers, and from evil. But salvation is also a matter of being saved from the just judgment of God (Romans 1:18–3:19). Many think that at the last judgment, God will balance the good things we do against the bad, but Christian faith completely rejects that idea. Nothing we can do is enough to reconcile us to God. Jesus Christ is the only ground, or basis, for salvation.

But we also need a broader, deeper, truer vision of what salvation means. Too often we focus on what we are saved *from*—sin, death, wrath, and hell. We need to think also about what we are saved *for*. We are saved to enter into a new family, the loving family of the church and the people of God. And at the heart of that, we can now call God "*Abba*, Father" as we receive the Spirit (Romans 8:15–16; Galatians 4:5–7). We are at one with God.

Too often we think of salvation in the very narrow terms of going to heaven when we die. But people today often ask, "Is there life before death?" And the glorious answer of the gospel is, "Yes!" Salvation gives us a sure hope for the age to come, but it also gives us sure hope for today. People make messes of their lives today. People are addicted to alcohol, drugs, tobacco, and pornography today. Families are divided today. The good news of the gospel is that people can know redemption and reconciliation today. The atonement of Christ is the ground for salvation today—liberty and peace and a new life.

That means that salvation includes present sanctification. The atonement does not only bring us salvation as pardon and justification; it also brings us salvation as purity and cleansing. "The blood of Jesus his Son cleanses us from all sin" (1 John 1:7b, NRSV).

John Wesley had some very stern words for a mentor of his, William Law, who had emphasized that he must "imitate" Christ but had said nothing about the atonement as the only ground of salvation. Wesley wrote: "Nor is there any more sure way to the imitation of Christ than faith in Christ crucified, in him who suffered for us. . . . The origin and cause of our redemption is the ineffable love of God the Father, who willed to redeem us by the blood of his Son; the grace of the Son, who freely took our curse upon him . . . and the Holy Spirit, who communicates the love of the Father and the grace of the Son to our hearts. When we speak of this and of the satisfaction of Christ, we speak of the inmost mystery of the Christian faith.[1]

Sufficient for Every Individual of Adam's Race

This phrase emphasizes the doctrine of universal atonement. That is the doctrine that Christ died for all, and it is quite explicit in various scriptural passages. Our mediator, Christ Jesus, "gave himself as a ransom for all" (1 Timothy 2:5–6; see also Hebrews 2:9; John 3:17; 12:47).

This doctrine must not be confused with universalism, the notion that all will be saved. Instead, it is emphasizing that those who are lost will be lost despite the fact that God longed for them to be saved and that Christ died for them.

It is necessary to clarify this point because some good, Bible-believing, God-honoring, Christian brothers and sisters believe in limited atonement—that Christ only died for the elect, those whom God predestined for salvation from the beginning. The great reformer John Calvin often affirmed that Christ died for all. But, out of a desire to glorify God and not to take any credit for his own salvation, he developed the doctrine that, before the foundation of the world, God elected part of the human race to salvation and "reprobated" the remainder to damnation. The elect would believe the gospel and be saved; those who were "reprobate" would not. Some of his followers (though not all) deduced that that must mean Christ died only for the elect. They then found ways of explaining away the texts of Scripture that did not fit their system.

John Wesley was horrified at the teaching of predestination to damnation and the teaching that Christ did not die for all. He regarded

---

1. John Wesley, Letters, vol. 3, 354.

it as a blasphemy against the love of God. He and his brother, Charles, regarded his Christian friends who taught this as seriously misled, and they emphasized again and again that Christ died for all.

For every man he tasted death.

He suffered once for all.

He calls as many souls as breathe,

And all may hear the call.

Thou canst not mock the sons of men,

Invite us to draw nigh,

Offer thy grace to all, and then

Thy grace to most deny!

Horror to think that God is hate!

Fury in God can dwell!

God would a helpless world create

To thrust them into hell!

—Charles Wesley

Children and Those Incapable of Moral Responsibility

Lastly, the Article of Faith on atonement speaks of those millions of human beings who are incapable of understanding the gospel. The atonement is "graciously efficacious" for their salvation (that is to say, it is effective). It produces their salvation. In short, they will be saved.

This point of doctrine is best viewed from the perspective of corporate atonement. Our usual phrase, "universal atonement," can still leave us thinking of the salvation of individuals. In almost all the debates in the modern era, we have thought of human beings only as individuals. Individualism is deeply ingrained in Western culture, so we tend to think of salvation and atonement only in individual terms. But biblical scholars draw our attention to the fact that biblical thinking begins by being much more corporate. The basic unit of humanity is not the individual; it is the family, the tribe, the body (*corpus*) of the human race as a whole. When the Son of God became incarnate, he became a member of that unity. He took "flesh" (John 1:14), the common physical basis for all human life. When he crucified the old humanity (Romans 6:6), the human race died corporately in him. When he rose from the dead, it was as the first fruits of the new humanity. In this way, he became the new head of the body (Colossians 1:18), the new humanity. The cross did not only create the possibility of salvation; it actually achieved salvation for the human race considered corporately. That is the basis for saying that infants and those who never come to moral responsibility will actually be saved.

Does this mean that all will be saved? Sadly, no. We have been reconciled, but those who hear and understand must each personally heed the call, "Be reconciled!" (2 Corinthians 5:18–20). As Article VI finally says, those who come to the age of responsibility must repent and believe. If they refuse, they will be "denying the sovereign Lord who bought them" (2 Peter 2:1). Our reconciliation with God has been achieved corporately; that is why we may each say with assurance when we gaze upon the cross, "My sins were canceled there at Calvary." The Lamb of God bore away the sin of the world (John 1:29). But while God has dealt with sin corporately, all who are able are called to enter in personally. His aim is a worldwide fellowship of persons who are at one with him, loving him as freely as he loves us.

Questions for Reflection or Discussion

Think about the material you have read in chapter 6 and consider your responses to the following questions. Use scriptural references to strengthen your answers whenever possible.

1. What is the difference between knowing about Jesus Christ and believing in him?

2. Why is a personal relationship with Jesus Christ such a vital aspect of the Christian faith?

3. What does the word *atonement* mean to you?

4. How is Jesus Christ's death on the cross a demonstration of his love for us?

5. How is Jesus Christ's death on the cross both a way of accounting for our disobedient rebellion against God and a way of restoring relationship with lost humanity?

6. Explain in simple terms how Jesus represented lost humanity on the cross.

7. How do you respond to the popular cultural notion that, at the end of life, God weighs all of our good deeds against our bad deeds and we go to heaven only if the good outweighs the bad?

8. What other misconceptions of salvation have you heard?

9. What does Jesus Christ save us *from* in his atoning death on the cross?

10. What does Jesus Christ save us *for* in his atoning death on the cross?

11. How does Christian salvation give us hope for today?

12. What do we mean when we say that atonement in Christ not only forgives us of past sins but also includes sanctification through purity and cleansing?

13. What do we mean when we say "Christ died for all" (see John 3:17; 12:47; 1 Timothy 2:5–6, Hebrews 2:9)?

14. How does the doctrine of universal atonement differ from universalism?

15. Why is universalism so popular today?

16. How does the doctrine of universal atonement differ from limited atonement?

17. Why is the doctrine of limited atonement so popular today?

18. How do we explain the certainty of salvation for infants, small children, and those who do not have moral responsibility?

19. Why are our repentance and belief important parts of understanding Christ's atonement?

20. How can we do a better job of explaining Christ's atonement to our needy world?

7 THE GRACE THAT PRECEDES

by Hunter Dale Cummings

Hunter Dale Cummings has a PhD from Nazarene Theological College in Manchester and serves as a lead pastor in Georgia.

VII. Prevenient Grace

7. We believe that the human race's creation in godlikeness included ability to choose between right and wrong, and that thus human beings were made morally responsible; that through the fall of Adam they became depraved so that they cannot now turn and prepare themselves by their own natural strength and works to faith and calling upon God. But we also believe that the grace of God through Jesus Christ is freely bestowed upon all people, enabling all who will to turn from sin to righteousness, believe on Jesus Christ for pardon and cleansing from sin, and follow good works pleasing and acceptable in his sight.

We believe that all persons, though in the possession of the experience of regeneration and entire sanctification, may fall from grace and apostatize and, unless they repent of their sins, be hopelessly and eternally lost.

(Genesis 1:26–27; 2:16–17; Deuteronomy 28:1–2; 30:19; Joshua 24:15; Job 14:4; 15:14; Psalms 8:3–5; 14:1–4; 51:5; Isaiah 1:8–10; Jeremiah 31:29–30; Ezekiel 18:1–4, 25–26; Micah 6:8; John 1:12–13; 3:6; Acts 5:31; Romans 1:19–20; 2:1–16; 3:10–12; 5:6–8, 12–14, 18, 20; 6:15–16, 23; 7:14–25; 10:6–8; 11:22; 14:7–12; 1 Corinthians 2:9–14; 10:1–12; 2 Corinthians 5:18–19; Galatians 5:6; 6:7–8; Ephesians 2:8–10; Philippians 2:12–13; Colossians 1:21–23; 2 Timothy 4:10; Titus 2:11–14; Hebrews 2:1–3; 3:12–15; 6:4–6; 10:26–31; James 2:18–22; 2 Peter 1:10–11; 2:20–22)

"How am I still alive?" she asked, shaking her head and smiling; and, with eyes glazing over, she began to reminisce over her life's journey. Brittany should have been dead. Steve, her pastor, knew she had almost died before he ever got to the hospital, but the pastor had no idea that Brittany had almost died a half a dozen times earlier in her life.

Pastor Steve answered her, "By the prevenient grace of God."

"What's prevenient grace?" she asked.

Grace that Goes Before

Prevenient grace, or preceding grace, is God's grace that goes before us. Biblically, the concept is suggested in the opening prologue of the gospel of John: "The true light that gives light to everyone was coming into the world" (John 1:9). Two basic components to prevenient grace are implied in this verse.

First, prevenient grace is given to everyone. This gift ties directly to our belief that Jesus Christ "made a full atonement for all human sin." Christ died for all, and God's gift of free grace is available for everyone who would receive it. Secondly, the light "was coming into the world." God has been pouring grace out into the world since the beginning and continues to do so.

Our growth in grace is a process, and while grace is given in the same measure to all, not all have the same capacity to understand the fullness of light they have been given. Evidences of prevenient grace abound in Scripture, but it comes to us from Christian tradition as well. Prevenient grace as a concept appears early in church history at the Second Synod of Orange in the sixth century, when it was decided that prevenient grace is necessary for the very beginning of faith. The idea also appears in the sixteenth century at the Council of Trent.

Prevenient grace also figures into orthodox Christianity. Orthodoxy teaches synergism (the interplay between human freedom and divine grace in our salvation). Yet Roman Catholicism and orthodoxy (Eastern and Western Christianity) do not subscribe to total depravity like the third major branch of Christianity, Protestantism. Early debates over Augustine's theology of humanity's free will gave way to the more nuanced debates of the seventeenth and eighteenth centuries between

53

Arminianism and Calvinism. Calvinism chooses to emphasize God's sovereign will and choice as the means to explain how total depravity is overcome for human beings. Arminians view prevenient grace as what enables us to overcome the effects of our total depravity.

Grace that Works behind the Scenes

Pastor Steve pointed out to Brittany how God's grace may have been working uniquely in her life, since a couple in their church had felt compelled to give Brittany a new car, with airbags, just a week before the accident. Prevenient grace means God sometimes acts on our behalf to keep us from harm's way. Pastor Steve believed that the kind of sacrificial giving evidenced by his parishioners was an expression of the grace of God in their hearts, just as was Brittany's salvation.

Brittany had started attending Pastor Steve's church only a few months after they met on the city bus route. Prevenient grace explains how God brings us into relationship with one another as well as how God draws us into community, specifically as God's people (the church). God's grace, Pastor Steve explained, had spared her in a way that the first responders called "truly miraculous." He told her God had been showing her mercy throughout every dark valley of her life leading up to the worship service in which she heard God calling her to repent and believe in Jesus Christ. Prevenient grace explains God's gracious actions, yes, but also God's calling.

Wesleyan scholar Albert Outler explained that prevenient grace can be construed in both a narrow and a broad sense. So far, Brittany's miracle has only illustrated the most narrow sense of prevenient grace. Outler says the narrow sense of prevenient grace is all about God's work in sinners' lives before they are saved (before justifying and sanctifying grace). Pastor Steve saw this in the miraculous events in which God saved Brittany's biological life. But as Brittany lay in her hospital bed and reflected on her hard life—and hard it was, for it had included drug addiction, an abusive relationship, a divorce, and repeated poor decisions—she realized that, even before she had made a decision to return to Christ after one of Pastor Steve's sermons, God had been leading her back home to God's people and a life committed to God's ways.

Grace that Enables

Yet prevenient grace can also broadly describe all grace because it describes God's prior activity. John Wesley's understanding of prevenient grace was broader than just conversations and decisions that led sinners closer to God. For Wesley, prevenient grace undoes the effects of original sin and the total depravity at the heart of the Protestant reformer's theology.

Kenneth Collins, in his book *The Theology of John Wesley*, suggests five effects that prevenient grace might have. Prevenient grace provides the following:

1. Basic knowledge of the attributes of God.

2. Re-inscription of the moral law.

3. Conscience formed by God, not just society or nature.

4. Measure of free will graciously restored.

5. Restraint of wickedness.

All of the above effects bring truth to the Gospel of John's claim that "the true light that gives light to everyone was coming into the world" (1:9). A one-word summary of all of these effects is "enabling." Prevenient or preceding grace may as well be described as enabling grace, for it enables us to do, in part, what total depravity previously made impossible.

Just then the nurse came into the room, smiling brightly.

"Who is this?" the nurse asked.

Brittany proudly said, "This is my pastor."

The nurse looked surprised and asked, "How in the world did you become a Christian?"

Brittany had already told the nurse some of the stories from her past experiences. Brittany's background and the first part of her life story did not seem to give the impression that she would have had her pastor visiting her or that she would be a Christian. Brittany laughed.

"It's a long story. We were just discussing how grace explains the most unlikely of conversion stories as well as the journey of those who are raised in the church."

After the nurse left, Brittany explained to Pastor Steve that she was struggling with how to go about witnessing to her nurse for Christ. Caroline was the most Jesus-like person she had ever met, but she wasn't a Christian and didn't have any interest in going to church, something Brittany discovered after making small talk with her and inviting Caroline to her church. Brittany asked Pastor Steve, "How do you reconcile the fact that Caroline seems more like Christ than some Christians?"

After pausing for a moment, Pastor Steve said, "Caroline reflects her Creator's mercy in the way she does her job. Even though she may not be a Christian, she can still experience God's prevenient grace in choosing to live a life of kindness."

"I don't understand," Brittany replied. "You taught me last week that we are all dead in our sins and that, before knowing Jesus, we cannot even choose the good that we want to choose. Remember that Bible study on Romans 7?"

Pastor Steve responded, "Well, before I decided to ask Jesus to save me from my sins, God graciously gave me a desire to want to obey him. Even when our wills are in bondage and we are not free to choose the good, God gives us free will to actually make a choice. Your nurse has been blessed with the ability to make a conscious decision to be kind to her patients."

Not only does enabling or prevenient grace explain the kindness of Brittany's nurse, but it also explains why those who have not even heard the name of Jesus can act with a conscience. Prevenient grace in human lives is one way that God restrains evil in a fallen world. Such a holistic doctrine is essential to a viable Christian worldview.

Grace without Limits

Every person has a worldview—a way in which they see or don't see God, humanity, and the direction the world is going. A feasible worldview does three things: It describes reality; it is internally coherent; and it is open to questions. Prevenient grace meets all of these expectations because it is limitless.

First, prevenient grace helps us to describe reality in all its complexity. It describes how those outside the body of Christ can accomplish so much good. It describes complicated, miraculous situations like Brittany's return to Christ as well as Brittany's miraculous free gift that saved her life.

Second, prevenient grace makes our theology internally coherent. It allows Wesleyans to hold in tension beliefs about total depravity, salvation by grace, human responsibility, and Christ's unlimited atonement.

Third, prevenient grace's limitless possibilities open us to ask tough questions of our Christian worldview. A robust theology of prevenient grace should open conversations to other religions, belief systems, and faith traditions. We must be careful to remember that this work in the world has a singular purpose. One does not turn the open sign on without a purpose.

Prevenient grace must not be confused with the grace that converts, justifies, saves, and sanctifies. Having someone pack our suitcase for a journey is not the same as actually starting the journey. Yet, once on the journey, this limitless grace of God gives pastors the humility to join recovering drug users in asking, "How am I still alive?"

The answer, in all cases, is prevenient grace.

Questions for Reflection or Discussion

Think about the material you have read in chapter 7 and consider your responses to the following questions. Use scriptural references to strengthen your answers whenever possible.

1. What does the notion of the prevenient grace of God mean to you?

2. Can you think of examples of the prevenient grace of God in your life?

3. How is prevenient grace a necessary component of our coming to faith in Christ?

4. How do you explain the relationship between human freedom and divine grace in our salvation?

5. How does a Wesleyan-Arminian understanding of prevenient grace, as understood in the Church of the Nazarene, differ from the Calvinist view of an extreme divine sovereign will?

6. What is an example of how God's prevenient grace keeps us from harm's way?

7. What is an example of how God's prevenient grace brings us into the community of faith?

8. What is an example of how God's prevenient grace calls us to God's self?

9. What is an example of how God's prevenient grace goes before us in a variety of ways in daily life?

10. What can we learn about God's attributes through prevenient grace?

11. What does prevenient grace teach us about God's moral law?

12. How does prevenient grace help shape our conscience?

13. How does prevenient grace help enable our free will?

14. What is an example of how God's prevenient grace enables us to overcome the damage of sin's depravity?

15. What is an example of how God's prevenient grace places within us the desire to want to obey God?

16. What is an example of how God's prevenient grace restrains evil in our fallen world?

17. How does God's prevenient grace help us describe reality in all its complexities?

18. How does God's prevenient grace make our theology internally coherent?

19. How does God's prevenient grace open us to ask tough questions of our Christian worldview?

20. Explain the difference between prevenient grace and the divine grace that converts, justifies, saves, and sanctifies us.

THE ONGOING NECESSITY

by Rubén Fernández

Rubén Fernández is rector of Seminario Nazareno de las Américas and regional education coordinator for the Mesoamerica Region.

VIII. Repentance

8. We believe that repentance, which is a sincere and thorough change of the mind in regard to sin, involving a sense of personal guilt and a voluntary turning away from sin, is demanded of all who have by act or purpose become sinners against God. The Spirit of God gives to all who will repent the gracious help of penitence of heart and hope of mercy, that they may believe unto pardon and spiritual life.

(2 Chronicles 7:14; Psalms 32:5–6; 51:1–17; Isaiah 55:6–7; Jeremiah 3:12–14; Ezekiel 18:30–32; 33:14–16; Mark 1:14–15; Luke 3:1–14; 13:1–5; 18:9–14; Acts 2:38; 3:19; 5:31; 17:30–31; 26:16–18; Romans 2:4; 2 Corinthians 7:8–11; 1 Thessalonians 1:9; 2 Peter 3:9)

"Please make the next legal U-turn," my GPS system insisted. But I didn't want to listen. I wanted to go my own way. I chose to disobey its good guidance, and that brought me consequences. I got lost!

Repentance is making a U-turn in life. It's a total change of direction. A 180-degree turnaround. You've reversed course; you're headed toward a new destination.

Repentance is not an attractive word in the postmodern era. You probably won't hear much about repentance in the media, even on popular Christian channels. It doesn't help the ratings. Nobody likes to be told they must repent. It's that way even in church services, where more "user-friendly" methods are sought for addressing the topic. Unfortunately, such practices do not get to the bottom of people's lives. The "whole counsel of God" is not proclaimed (Acts 20:27, NKJV).

Jesus Preached Repentance

Jesus was a preacher of repentance. Mark 1:15 tells us that his message had three simple points: "The time has come. . . .The kingdom of God has come near. Repent and believe the good news."

On his way to Jerusalem, Jesus used two tragic events to call his fellow citizens to repent. People often interpreted disasters or accidents as punishment for some sin that "worse sinners" had committed in the past. But Jesus said no, everyone should repent, or perish (Luke 13:2–3).

In chapter 15 of the same Gospel, Jesus told three beautiful parables about the shepherd who found his lost sheep, the woman who found her lost coin, and the father who forgave his lost son. In the first two parables, Jesus revealed the intimacy of heaven celebrating a single human being's repentance (vv. 7, 10). The third parable shows us clearly the steps in the repentance of the Prodigal Son: waking up to the facts, realizing the situation (v. 17); deciding to change (v. 18); turning around, moving in the right direction (v. 20); and humbly asking for forgiveness (v. 21).

The Fruit of Repentance

The message of repentance that Jesus preached was taken up by the early church. We see this with Peter at Pentecost (Acts 2) and Philip in his encounter with the Ethiopian (Acts 8). In Athens, Paul cleverly conveyed the message of the gospel, clearly telling the Greeks that they must repent (Acts 17:30).

Repentance involves the conviction that we have offended God. In addition, for there to be repentance, there must be a deep sorrow for our sins and a change of attitude. There should be a clear decision to abandon sin and to demonstrate this decision through fruits of repentance. If this follow-up does not happen, repentance is not genuine. That is why unrepentant believers can be found in the membership lists of Christian churches.

Paul said that, for those who are in Christ, "the old has gone" (2 Corinthians 5:17). The Greek word translated "gone" also means "stopped being" or "disappeared," and the verb is in the *aorist* tense, indicating that it is a definitive act, once and for all. Interestingly, it is the same term used to mean drastic changes in creation, at the end of time: For example, Luke 21:33 says, "Heaven and earth will pass away, but my words will never pass away." In 2 Peter 3, the "day of the Lord" is described like this: "The heavens will disappear with a roar; the elements will be destroyed by fire, and the earth and everything done in it will be laid bare" (v. 10).

To repent, we need to have an inner desire that first comes from the grace of God (Romans 2:4). Although it is true that the Spirit gives us the power to make the change, the final decision is entirely ours.

Repentance and Renewal

To grow in the Christian life, we need to be attentive to the voice of the Holy Spirit when he shows us we are wrong in our thinking or in something we have said or done. Repenting means giving up the sinful practices of the old life, which prepares us for a renewal in all areas of our lives by the Spirit. Even David—the king after God's own heart— was a ruler who had to repent for his sin (Psalm 51). Pastors and churches sometimes need to repent, as seen in the churches at Ephesus, Pergamum, Thyatira, Sardis, and Laodicea (Revelation 2 and 3).

Sometimes, Christians need to change their attitude, as Peter did in Acts 10. Peter at first believed that only Jews could be saved, but by the hand of God Peter got his chance to change—and change he did. He shared his "aha" moment in the house of Cornelius, the Roman centurion, when he said, "I now realize how true it is that God does not show favoritism but accepts from every nation the one who fears him and does what is right" (Acts 10:34–35). Peter was transformed in his thinking. We see it in the fact that, when the Holy Spirit came upon Cornelius and those who were with him, Peter commanded them to be baptized. We see it again in the report that Peter gave to the church in Jerusalem, narrated in Acts 2.

In Repentance

We all need those pivotal moments in our lives. They come as a result of reading the Word, praying, listening to preaching, studying the Bible, listening to other people, or—as in the case of Peter—in other creative ways the Holy Spirit uses.

The need for repentance is a permanent part of the Christian life, even for sanctified Christians. The Holy Spirit leads us to maturity and shows us the areas in our lives that need to change. To persevere in a holy life, we need to be alert to the Spirit's voice and correct our course when he tells us something is wrong.

The apostle John reminds us that, when we remain in Christ, the blood of Jesus continues to purify us from all sin (1 John 1:7). Christians cannot escape temptation, but we can resist it by the grace of God operating in our lives. First Corinthians 10:12 reminds us of an important truth: "So, if you think you are standing firm, be careful that you don't fall!"

In Philippians 1:6 Paul said, "Being confident of this, that he who began a good work in you will carry it on to completion until the day of Christ Jesus." In the Christian life, there is always the need to be careful not to go astray, as expressed in Hebrews 2:1: "We must pay the most careful attention, therefore, to what we have heard, so that we do not drift away."

The Holy Spirit is our GPS in the spiritual life. We must listen carefully to his voice and follow his instructions when he says, "Make a U-turn!"

Questions for Reflection or Discussion

Think about the material you have read in chapter 8 and consider your responses to the following questions. Use scriptural references to strengthen your answers whenever possible.

1. How do you define repentance?

2. What are some important biblical principles used to explain the concept of repentance?

3. Why did Jesus preach the unpopular message of repentance?

4. Why must we repent before we can believe the good news of Jesus's message?

5. Why is it as easy today as it was in Jesus's day to judge people who are "worse" sinners than we think we are and refuse to see our own need for God's forgiveness?

6. Give an example from your own experience, or the experience of someone you know, for each of the steps Jesus gave toward repentance in the parable of the Prodigal Son (Luke 15):
   • Waking up to the facts
   • Realizing the situation
   • Deciding to change
   • Turning around
   • Moving in the right direction
   • Humbly asking for forgiveness

7. How do we offend God and stand in need of repentance?

8. Why must we sorrow over our sins and have a change of attitude toward them?

9. Why must we determine to abandon our sins in order to have genuine repentance?

10. Once we have repented of our sins, why can we not simply return to a regular practice of conscience-free sinning, as some believe?

11. How does the Holy Spirit empower us to repent?

12. Name ways the Holy Spirit calls us to repentance through:
    - Reading the Bible
    - Listening to sermons
    - Listening to the testimony of other Christians
    - Praying for God's leadership

13. In what areas of life does the Holy Spirit call upon sanctified believers to repent?

14. Why must believers remain open to the voice of the Holy Spirit calling for repentance?

15. How might a resistance to the voice of the Spirit lead a believer to fall into temptation?

16. What dangers exist in the Christian life that lead to spiritual drifting from God's will and direction for our lives?

17. How do we best resist the temptation to drift from God's will and direction for our lives?

18. Why is the Holy Spirit so eager to prompt believers to continue walking in the right direction?

19. What is an example from your own life, or the experience of someone you know, of the Holy Spirit's guiding voice to repent of sin or face new light?

20. How do we best nurture the guiding voice of the Holy Spirit in our lives?

A GRACIOUS NEW START

by Samantha Chambo

Samantha Chambo is an ordained elder in the Church of the Nazarene and coordinator of Africa Nazarene Women Clergy.

IX. Justification, Regeneration, and Adoption

9. We believe that justification is the gracious and judicial act of God by which he grants full pardon of all guilt and complete release from the penalty of sins committed, and acceptance as righteous, to all who believe on Jesus Christ and receive him as Lord and Savior.

9.1. We believe that regeneration, or the new birth, is that gracious work of God whereby the moral nature of the repentant believer is spiritually quickened and given a distinctively spiritual life, capable of faith, love, and obedience.

9.2. We believe that adoption is that gracious act of God by which the justified and regenerated believer is constituted a [child] of God.

9.3. We believe that justification, regeneration, and adoption are simultaneous in the experience of seekers after God and are obtained upon the condition of faith, preceded by repentance; and that to this work and state of grace the Holy Spirit bears witness.

(Luke 18:14; John 1:12–13; 3:3–8; 5:24; Acts 13:39; Romans 1:17; 3:21–26, 28; 4:5–9, 17–25; 5:1, 16–19; 6:4; 7:6; 8:1, 15–17; 1 Corinthians 1:30; 6:11; 2 Corinthians 5:17–21; Galatians 2:16–21; 3:1–14, 26; 4:4–7; Ephesians 1:6–7; 2:1, 4–5; Philippians 3:3–9; Colossians 2:13; Titus 3:4–7; 1 Peter 1:23; 1 John 1:9; 3:1–2, 9; 4:7; 5:1, 9–13, 18)

As a little girl, I often envied my friends who came from stable homes. Because my own home was rather turbulent, I imagined the great life I would have had if I had been born into a different home. Now, as an adult, I am thankful for the biological family I was born into, but I am eternally thankful that I did receive a new spiritual family that enabled me to have a great new life. This is a result of my salvation. The Church of the Nazarene's Article of Faith IX expresses the wonderful change that happens in us when we enter into a relationship with Jesus Christ. It is the beginning of a new and liberated life.

Justification: A Clean State

When we think of justification, we are reminded of a loving God who went to great lengths to bring us into a right relationship with himself. He did this by sending his Son to die on the cross on our behalf. We are set free from punishment because Jesus Christ took our place on the cross. As a result, we can be free from fear of judgment and condemnation, and we can also have freedom from feelings of guilt and shame that are generally the glue that keeps us stuck to our old ways of life. We can enjoy the fact that Jesus Christ, in his death and resurrection, gained victory over sin on our behalf, and we can live victorious lives by God's grace. Guilt, fear, and shame cut us off from God and others because we don't feel worthy of their love. But God's gracious gift gives us a new start. Justification means we get a clean slate to start over. In justification we are declared not guilty, which means we can live in God's presence with a clean conscience. We receive this justification as a free gift from God when we choose to respond to God's faithful love to us by believing in his Son. J. A. Motyer said, "Just as in the beginning God said, 'Let there be light,' and there was light so, at the moment he appointed for our new birth, he said, 'Let there be life,' and there was life."

Regeneration: New Spiritual Life

Regeneration gives us new spiritual life, which means we now have a new sensitivity to God's Holy Spirit, and we have better moral discernment. We don't have to live by the script of sin, or in self-centeredness, or under the control of negative things that happen to us. We can choose to be free from predetermined responses and to live according to the Holy Spirit's direction in our lives. Regeneration also means the cleaning out of old negatives in our lives and gaining an increased capacity to love God and others.

Although justification and regeneration happen simultaneously, they are distinct gifts. In justification I am brought into a new relationship with God and given a chance at a new, wonderful life, but in regeneration I am prepared, equipped, and renewed to be able to live this new life. This is what 2 Corinthians 5:17 says about justification: "Therefore, if anyone is in Christ, the new creation has come: The old has gone, the new is here!"

H. O. Wiley said, "By justification, God takes us into his favor; by adoption, into his heart."

Adoption: Belonging and Support

Adoption provides belonging and the support system to live this new life. I am a new person in a new family. I am accepted as one of God's children with all the privileges, benefits, and responsibilities. In Romans 8:1–17, Paul says we are adopted into God's family and that we now have the right to call God "*Abba*, Father"—a very intimate way of referring to God. Paul teaches in Romans 8 that we are now co-heirs with Jesus Christ. But he also states the responsibility we have as members of God's family. We should live in obedience to the Spirit of God. This obedience is made possible by the work of regeneration by the same Spirit in our lives.

Hanging around with an old crowd is difficult because they expect you to behave according to your old ways. Being part of God's family provides me with a new environment where I can thrive as God's child. This does not mean I will be cut off from my blood relatives. It does mean that God has provided a new family for me, who share the same beliefs as I do, who understand and love me, accept me, and encourage the new me to live completely for God. The newly shared family rituals such as baptism, the Lord's Supper, and communal worship are all signs of my new place in God's holy family.

Just the Start

So in justification, regeneration, and adoption we are: brought into a right relationship with God; loved, accepted, and forgiven; given new life that is the start of continual transformation in our lives; and received into a new family where our transformation is nurtured. All of these happen simultaneously and are all part of one, wonderful blessing.

The best part of all this is that this new life is just the start of an ever-deepening relationship with Christ as I am transformed to be more like him. Although it is a once-and-for-all work that God does in and for me at my conversion, it is an ongoing blessing. This means that my relationships with God and others are continually adjusted. Both as I grow or as I commit errors out of my human weakness, I am being made alive every day. I grow in my knowledge of Christ and am established as part of the family of God as I learn to trust Christ more.

The practical outflow of this change affects my relationships with those outside the church as well. It is impossible for one who has received such lavish love and grace to hoard it selfishly. So my greatest joy becomes inviting other people into this wonderful family of God. Being accepted into God's family has saved my life in more than one way, and for that I am eternally grateful.

Questions for Reflection or Discussion

Think about the material you have read in chapter 9 and consider your responses to the following questions. Use scriptural references to strengthen your answers whenever possible.

1. The word *justification* comes from the courtroom, when a judge declares someone on trial not guilty. How does this word apply to our spiritual justification through God's declaration?

2. How would you explain justification in simple terms to a friend?

3. How can God declare sinners not guilty and remain faithful to God's own nature, which is holy and righteous?

4. The word *regeneration* means something is made new again, or new birth. How does this word apply to our spiritual lives, which have been touched by God?

5. How would you explain regeneration in simple terms to a friend?

6. How are justification and regeneration different?

7. The word *adoption* relates to family relationships. How does this word apply to our change in relationship with God?

8. How is the Christian concept of adopted children being brought into close relationship with the heavenly Father different from the religions of the world that have no concept of a familial relationship with their god(s)?

9. In what ways does the community of faith become a believer's new family?

10. How is our faith family like our biological family?

11. How is our faith family different from our biological family?

12. In what ways does God change believers over time to be more like Christ?

13. What Christian practices help us remain open to God changing us over time to be more like Christ?

14. What is the difference between sinfulness and human weakness?

15. Will believers ever be delivered from all human weakness in this life?

16. Describe in your own words what it feels like to hear God declare you "not guilty!"

17. Describe in your own words how regeneration has changed your life through God's regenerating power.

18. Describe in your own words what it felt like to be adopted into the family of God.

19. What motivates Christians to invite others to experience God through justification, regeneration, and adoption?

20. How does God empower us to live lives that testify to God's justifying, regenerating, and adopting work?

10 UPWARD, INWARD, AND OUTWARD

by Deirdre Brower Latz

Deirdre Brower Latz is the principal and senior lecturer in pastoral and social theology at Nazarene Theological College in Manchester, England.

X. Christian Holiness and Entire Sanctification

10. **We believe that sanctification is the work of God which transforms believers into the likeness of Christ. It is wrought by God's grace through the Holy Spirit in initial sanctification, or regeneration (simultaneous with justification), entire sanctification, and the continued perfecting work of the Holy Spirit culminating in glorification. In glorification we are fully conformed to the image of the Son.**

We believe that entire sanctification is that act of God, subsequent to regeneration, by which believers are made free from original sin, or depravity, and brought into a state of entire devotement to God, and the holy obedience of love made perfect.

It is wrought by the baptism with or infilling of the Holy Spirit, and comprehends in one experience the cleansing of the heart from sin and the abiding, indwelling presence of the Holy Spirit, empowering the believer for life and service.

Entire sanctification is provided by the blood of Jesus, is wrought instantaneously by grace through faith, preceded by entire consecration; and to this work and state of grace the Holy Spirit bears witness.

This experience is also known by various terms representing its different phases, such as "Christian perfection," "perfect love,"

"heart purity," "the baptism with or infilling of the Holy Spirit," "the fullness of the blessing," and "Christian holiness."

10.1 We believe that there is a marked distinction between a pure heart and a mature character. The former is obtained in an instant, the result of entire sanctification; the latter is the result of growth in grace.

We believe that the grace of entire sanctification includes the divine impulse to grow in grace as a Christlike disciple. However, this impulse must be consciously nurtured, and careful attention given to the requisites and processes of spiritual development and improvement in Christlikeness of character and personality. Without such purposeful endeavor, one's witness may be impaired and the grace itself frustrated and ultimately lost.

Participating in the means of grace, especially the fellowship, disciplines, and sacraments of the church, believers grow in grace and in wholehearted love to God and neighbor.

(Deuteronomy 30:6; Jeremiah 31:31–34; Ezekiel 36:25–27; Malachi 3:2–3; Matthew 3:11–12; 5:1–7:29; 22:37–40; Luke 3:16–17; John 7:37–39; 14:15–23; 15:1–11; 17:6–20; Acts 1:5; 2:1–4; 15:8–9; Romans 6:11–13, 19; 8:1–4, 8–14; 12:1–15:3; 15:29; 1 Corinthians 13; 2 Corinthians 6:14–7:1; Galatians 2:20; 5:16–25; Ephesians 3:14–21; 4:17–5:20; 5:25–27; Philippians 1:9–11; 3:10–15; Colossians 2:20–3:17; 1 Thessalonians 3:13; 4:7–8; 5:23–24; 2 Timothy 2:19–22; Hebrews 4:9–11; 6:1; 10:10–17, 19–25; 12:1–2, 14; 13:12, 20–21; 1 Peter 1:15–16, 22; 2 Peter 1:1–11; 3:18; 1 John 1:7, 9; 3:3; 4:17–18; Jude 20–21)

What does it mean to be one who affirms and embodies God's work of sanctification? God's holy people, made holy by God's Holy Spirit, re-sembling nothing more than God's holy One? Why does this matter for our everyday lives? Whenever I find myself considering what it means to be wholly holy, or fully God's child, I am drawn to three different, complex, and interwoven realities.

Upward

The only way imaginable for holiness to be all-consuming in our lives is for our lives to be wholly given to God. God's lavish and abundant firstness in loving us pours God's love upon us, and such initiating love beckons us to respond. God's love is compelling, and when believers respond—in a moment, and over a lifetime—they come to know more of what it means to be alive; fully, wholly, consumed by God's grace for them. They know themselves to be free, beloved, and whole. God's love begins to saturate their lives.

The more we participate in such a life of love, the more we discover we need deepening in our whole-hearted, life-saturated love of God as it fills and purifies us, witnessing to God's power at work in us by the Spirit of the living Lord Jesus. This participation has a beginning, but it does not have an ending. The witness of God's dwelling in my life (or yours), then, should be light-infusing and life-giving. Any stench of death-bringing, hateful, violent, disease will waft away. Instead we find life, newly created by God, that is fragrant, grace-filled and generous, deeply loving and love-saturated, committed, and godly in wisdom and counsel. The person who is drawn by the Spirit and responds to living in the way of Jesus gives God a yes to his or her life being remade, from the inside out and the outside in. It has been said not only do we think our way into acting but also act our way into thinking.

Our lives in their God-ness demonstrate repeatedly that God's ways are of love, mercy, forgiveness, justice, generosity, sacrifice, humility, and servant-hearted strength. Our lives must be lived in response to all that Christ has done—worked out in faithful commitment to the commands to love God, others, and self in the power of the Spirit. What God has done for us in Christ through the Spirit is worked out in us. Of course, the closer we are to God, the more aware we are of our immense reliance on God's Spirit to shape and renew us, form us, and infuse us so that we are entirely God's. Empowered by the Spirit, we lean on God's presence to form in us mature and holy characters with a distinct family resemblance to Jesus.

Inward

The truth will be worked out personally and corporately. The best evidence of a life of holiness will be gathered in multiple dimensions as we love God in praise and celebration and personally participate in disciplines and sacraments of the church and as we lead lives of daily, cross-shaped living. Our inward renewal is expressed in our love toward others—those treasured and valued people whom God loves and longs to draw into God's family, including people within the community of faith and outside of it; poor people, oppressed people, other people. In meeting with others not yet in community as well as with those in community, we quickly discover the ways we still need to align ourselves with grace. Nothing challenges holiness more than other people and their ways. Of course, in church we're to be participants in the kind of community that stretches you, truth-tells to you (and with you)—the kind of community that knows so much of grace that it oozes into the streets and regions around it. Yet, even these are tough places to hone holiness. But where there's a holiness community, lives are (should be) joyfully transformed, communities (should) begin to look different, the world sees (should see) that God's creative, life-giving love is always spilling into the highways and byways, inviting others to a feast.

In the day-to-day living out of holiness, God's life in us is breathed into and out of us in the rhythm of prayer, in disciplines of time, in restful abiding, in repeated acts of obedience, in mastering our tongues as we speak, in witnessing within us that God's presence is at work. It means the inner being is renewed—we, God's people, by one sacrifice, are being recreated into the image of Christ, God's only Son.

In our rhythms and practices of life, we gather as God's people, setting aside time to learn in community as the people of God. We remember our baptism and share in the Lord's Supper and are renewed in our spirit as people and individuals by the presence of the risen Christ through his Spirit in our midst. We feast together. We give of our time, money, energy; we offer our children up to this community of love, and we do so with open hearts, knowing that somehow or other we become more when we gather than when we are on our own. In our corporate practices we think of ourselves as we ought—neither better than others, nor unforgiven or forsaken. Remembering our forgiveness, we proclaim our joyful hope to those we encounter in friendship and in the ordinary places our lives take us. Hospitably, we hang out with people who don't yet know Jesus and trust that God's presence at work will help us find ways of seasoned conversations that speak of Jesus.

When we come to recognize and celebrate the gift of grace to us, we are discipled by other, wiser, mature people who journey with us, not perfectly flawless nor flawlessly perfect, but fully human people who wrestle with God's call and are renamed God's children, heirs: God's.

In our daily lives, from waking to sleeping, we seek God's face. From our private spaces where no one watches to our public spaces where we speak life and blessing over others, we increase in love. Our hearts ache for brokenness, for it is manifestly around us (and affects us). But, like the Jesus we know and love, we grieve for broken and pain-filled lives—and long to weep, then heal, then give our lives for the sake of others. We recognize where we fall short, and we confess, aware of our shortcomings and failures, and are willing to acknowledge them. We resist hate in all its forms, from racial to sexual, from bigotry that makes enemies of people, to hating our own selves. We resist hating, despising, or dismissing those not like us, and we search for God's eyesight to become our own: How does God's love color the community around us? How might we proclaim the reconciling power of cross-shaped love? How might our lives become more and more Christlike?

Outward

Compelled by the witness of a life lived out utterly and completely in service to God, this kind of whole-life consecration is beautiful to see. People touched by this holiness discover that it is contagious. It beckons to them. They want to be with these kind of holy people because their love of life is evident, their love of people is warming, their hope for others is inspiring, and their passionate belief that God is for others is a measure of their understanding of holiness.

Like Jesus, people in all their frailty discover that God's love is for the sick and sinning—and that, when God in Christ demands action (to sin no more), that same God gives strength for that self-same obedience and renewal. New brothers and sisters who come into faith are adopted into God's family as they are, and God's call to holy living is celebrated and embraced because of God's great gift of love and enabling grace, living out of that loving embrace, secure in the promises that God is able. Of course, I'm aware that such holiness is challenging and takes total cooperation with God's Spirit. And so, woven into our lives of holiness is a consecration, over and again speaking yes to God's direction of our lives. Open-hearted to rebuke, open-eared to exhortation, open-minded to learning, open-eyed to grace's works.

We are not afraid to name sin and failure, for only in so doing can we see that our denials of Christ (like Peter's) are outmatched by God's desire to forgive and offer renewal, transformed minds, living sacrifices. As Marva Dawn says, we realize that the problem with living sacrifices is that they crawl off the altar, and we determine that, by grace, we will renew daily our prayer for the bread of life.

We celebrate, though! For there is optimism in grace. God's Holy Spirit, the breath of life within us, enables us to be aligned with the plumb line of God's grace for humankind over and again. We realize that we do not have to succumb to sin's temptation, and we are wise enough to realize that temptation itself is not sin. Instead, when our lives are saturated by love, we do not leave room for sins of pride, hate, bitterness, cruelty. Even so, we are dynamic, frail, growing, maturing—true humans—and so our love needs to be practiced day to day.

Our lives given over to God mean so much more than a static, once-only response. Thank God that we become more and more Christlike as we imitate those who've gone before us. In this understanding of people wholly given to God, light-shining lives, personally and corporately reshaped into the likeness of Christ, we discover the profound hope that our faith offers us: Jesus is Lord and, as Lord, does more than we could ever imagine. So our holiness is dynamic, unhurried, fluid. It is a way of life, and the direction of our travel is toward its final culmination at the feast of the King, who sits and shares a meal of love with his good and faithful servants.

Questions for Reflection or Discussion

Think about the material you have read in chapter 10 and consider your responses to the following questions. Use scriptural references to strengthen your answers whenever possible.

1. What do the words *holiness* and *sanctification* mean to you?

2. In your opinion, what does it mean to be wholly dedicated to God?

3. How does our complete surrender compare to God's gift of his Son for our salvation?

4. Why does our participation in God's love have no end?

5. What practical application can you make to illustrate God's love as light-infusing and life-giving?

6. Why is wholehearted consecration to God essential for God's gift of entire sanctification?

7. How does God's love for us make us more like Christ in our love, mercy, forgiveness, justice, generosity, sacrifice, humility, and servant-hearted strength?

8. How do we lean on God's presence in ways that enable God to form in us mature and holy characters with a distinct family resemblance to Jesus?

9. Why do we call entire sanctification a gift from God?

10. What spiritual disciplines and sacraments of the church does God use to make us more like Christ?

11. Why is loving people both within the community of faith and outside of it important to God's sanctifying work in our hearts?

12. Why is this kind of love sometimes hard to display?

13. How do we celebrate God's gifts of grace within the community of faith?

14. Why is it important for holiness people to acknowledge when they fall short, confess it, and remain aware of shortcomings and failures?

15. How is wholehearted consecration to God contagious?

16. Why does God call his holy people to action in reaching lost and needy people?

17. Why is daily renewal of our total commitment to God a necessary part of growth in grace?

18. How does a life of sanctification enable us to resist the temptation to sin?

19. How does God's love at work in us expel sin from our hearts and lives?

20. In what ways does God's work of sanctification make us more like Christ?

BEING THE CHURCH
by Mónica Mastronardi de Fernández

Mónica Mastronardi de Fernández is the vice rector of institutional development at Seminario Nazareno de las Américas in Costa Rica.

XI. The Church

11. **We believe in the church, the community that confesses Jesus Christ as Lord, the covenant people of God made new in Christ, the body of Christ called together by the Holy Spirit through the Word.**

God calls the church to express its life in the unity and fellowship of the Spirit; in worship through the preaching of the Word, observance of the sacraments, and ministry in his name; by obedience to Christ, holy living, and mutual accountability.

The mission of the church in the world is to share in the redemptive and reconciling ministry of Christ in the power of the Spirit. The church fulfills its mission by making disciples through evangelism, education, showing compassion, working for justice, and bearing witness to the kingdom of God.

The church is a historical reality that organizes itself in culturally conditioned forms, exists both as local congregations and as a universal body, and also sets apart persons called of God for specific ministries. God calls the church to live under his rule in anticipation of the consummation at the coming of our Lord Jesus Christ.

(Exodus 19:3; Jeremiah 31:33; Matthew 8:11; 10:7; 16:13–19, 24; 18:15–20; 28:19–20; John 17:14–26; 20:21–23; Acts 1:7–8; 2:32–47; 6:1–2; 13:1; 14:23; Romans 2:28–29; 4:16; 10:9–15; 11:13–32; 12:1–8; 15:1–3; 1 Corinthians 3:5–9; 7:17; 11:1, 17–33; 12:3, 12–31; 14:26–40; 2 Corinthians 5:11–6:1; Galatians 5:6, 13–14; 6:1–5, 15; Ephesians 4:1–17; 5:25–27; Philippians 2:1–16; 1 Thessalonians 4:1–12; 1 Timothy 4:13; Hebrews 10:19–25; 1 Peter 1:1–2, 13; 2:4–12, 21; 4:1–2, 10–11; 1 John 4:17; Jude 24; Revelation 5:9–10)

Extreme sports are very popular. We seek to escape routine by experiencing something as challenging as swimming with sharks or co-piloting a fighter jet. People hate to feel bored.

While the church isn't called to stage bungee jumps or survival challenges in the jungle, being part of a "community that confesses Jesus Christ as Lord" should, nonetheless, be far from boring. In fact, participating in the church should be a vibrant, exciting, and challenging experience for all disciples of Jesus Christ.

The Church Has Only One Lord

Though people can be wary of the human institution we call the church, we need to recognize that the church does not have a human origin, nature, or purpose. The Bible provides us with an example of a living church, incarnated in history, faithfully following the example of the Lord, and acting to transform the world. The church is God's design; God is its Creator. As Paul teaches in Ephesians 5:25, Jesus Christ paid the price so the church could be established and developed in this world. The Holy Spirit is the church's builder, providing the materials (new believers, leadership, gifts) to help this building to grow and develop to the full potential of its capabilities, fulfilling the purpose for which it was designed (Acts 1:8).

We believe in a church that, like its Lord, uses the weapons of faith, peace, truth, justice, and the proclamation of the message of hope to destroy the powers of evil (Ephesians 6:14–17). However, the church pays a high price to advance the gospel. Throughout the world, people are killed every day solely because they are Christians. Currently, Christians in more than sixty countries are persecuted, imprisoned, tortured, or killed due to their faithful following of Jesus Christ. The world rejects the church because the church, putting on the armor of God (Ephesians 6:10–13), does not bow down to the powers of this world, nor does it cringe before the spiritual forces of evil. It is made up of the people of God who are born of the Spirit (John 3:6) and who live under the laws and values of the kingdom of God, not negotiating or assimilating the sinful customs of society but, rather, living in holiness (Ephesians 5:27) and in obedience to Christ. As Christ teaches in Mathew 5:13–16, the church is light and salt.

The Church Loves

Christians must first love the Lord and, second, love the family of God because loving God with all our hearts means embracing God's mission and family, and making them our own. To love the church means joining it.

The church "expresses its life in unity," and this communion, wrought by the Holy Spirit, can be easily broken if it is not cared for and nurtured. For the church to live in unity, we must eliminate all attitudes, words, or conduct that harm others and, instead, be proactive in showing love through relationships and in giving encouragement through positive conversation. Nothing is more damaging to the church than Christians who complain about or speak ill of their brothers, sisters, and leaders. Although in local churches as well as at other levels of the denomination there will always be room for improving relations and issues, complaining will not solve anything. Changes will only occur when we pray and put these situations in the hands of the Lord and, as he leads us, become involved positively and actively as part of the solution.

God designed the church as a place of communion, where there is healing of wounds and continued growth in the knowledge and love of God and others. The expressions of this unity are diverse, as shared in Hebrews 10:24–25: we need to pray together, intercede for one another, share food, enjoy each other's company, partake of the sacraments, share experiences and struggles, encourage each other, give good advice, and comfort and build each other up in the Word.

God's love unites the church and fills the lives of his children, who are then filled with the Holy Spirit. The Spirit teaches us to love God and our neighbor with a love that is impossible without his grace: an extreme and unlimited love. (See Matthew 18:15–22.)

The Church Spreads Life

Just as Jesus did, the church is called to give its life, to sacrifice so that individuals and families come to salvation and are restored to abundant life in Jesus Christ. The church, through the proclamation of the word of truth, exposes the powers of evil, which are hidden in the structures of injustice and oppression. It does not ignore suffering but stands as a defender, fighting to restore all creation, especially to the helpless, those who are invisible in this world. Every day the church struggles to minimize poverty, ignorance, disease, and all sorts of suffering and injustice.

For those who come from a Christian family, the church, rather than a mere community, is our extended family. There we have grandparents, aunts, cousins, parents, and siblings in the faith who love us and who are interested in our welfare. However, thanks be to God, this is not just true of those who have grown up in a community of faith; everyone can experience the church as a family.

Recently, in a baptismal service in Barrio Los Ángeles, San José, Costa Rica, baptism candidates shared stories of lives that touched the entire congregation. A young man of nineteen, who had come to the church the year prior, talked about the loneliness he had experienced since childhood, suffering verbal abuse from his stepfather. Holding back his tears, he stressed that when he arrived at the church he felt loved and accepted for the first time in his life. In the church he found the love of family that he had always longed for. Then an older woman said she had sought all her life to feel loved and accepted. Her bad decisions led her to a life of sin and vice, but her story changed completely when she came to the church. In the church she found love and acceptance, and through discipleship, she found guidance to redirect her life and follow Jesus Christ. Within a year, her situation completely changed, and now her dream is to train and use her gifts to win other women for Christ.

Our lives, our histories, consist of a progression of experiences. Some of them are unexpected, but most of these experiences are the product of our choices. The decision to join the church of Jesus Christ is one of the most important and crucial life decisions someone can make. It is an extreme decision that will forever transform one's life, giving it a new purpose and a new direction.

Live the Extreme Experience of Being the Church

To live the extreme experience of being the church, we have to get involved in what God is doing in the world to transform the lives of every child, young person, adult, and senior citizen forever. To engage in God's mission is the most challenging life dynamic that anyone can propose to us.

Today, many Christians need to change the way they see the church. God did not create the church to be one more activity in our lives but, rather, to engage us in transformational and exciting experiences. The beautiful event of accepting Christ as Savior is not the only vibrant experience that God has prepared for his children. The Christian life does not have to become routine and boring. When we look at the life of Jesus and the Christians of the early church, or when we read the biographies of great Christians who preceded us, we can say that their lives were far from boring; they were full of excitement and purpose.

Everyone who belongs to the church of the Lord shares the same vocation: "to work for justice and bear witness to the kingdom of God" in this world, promoting the kingdom of God in our midst, shedding light over darkness, risking being different, living in holiness, and being like Christ in the midst of a society that is sinking deeper into sin and knowing less and less about God. This is our great challenge.

Is it possible to change the world? Yes, but we need to commit ourselves with all our being to working together as the church: First, we need to cry out in constant and passionate prayer for family, friends, and acquaintances who are lost. Second, we must open our hearts by making friends with unbelievers, sharing Christ with them, and teaching them to live in holiness as disciples of Jesus. Third, our task is to train them and integrate them into the ministry of the church so that they too may become agents of change in their communities.

The church was designed to be the body of Christ (Ephesians 5:23). The call of the Lord is clear: God can only use a church that surrenders completely to his perfect will (Romans 12:1; Ephesians 5:2). God calls each and every one to serve in a specific place, both in the church and in the world, creatively using the gifts, skills, financial resources, and time he gives us. The best way to combat routine and boredom is to identify our gifts and then perfect and use them—and, in doing this, we will never be bored.

Serving the Lord is a life full of expectation, with exciting and surprising experiences. We are called to live the extreme experience of being actively involved in the church of Christ. The Lord invites us to be part of his wonderful plan, a project where we can grow and be improved continuously, where we can strive to the limit and give back to God everything good and wonderful that the Creator has placed in us. This is a project that will not end with our lives but will remain for eternity in every person who is rescued from the chains of sin. Let us not be mere spectators; instead, let us work together as the church living this extreme experience of participating with Jesus as he transforms the world.

Questions for Reflection or Discussion

Think about the material you have read in chapter 11 and consider your responses to the following questions. Use scriptural references to strengthen your answers whenever possible.

1. What is your definition of the church?

2. In what ways is participating in the church like participating in an extreme sport?

3. Why did God provide the church for believers and the world?

4. In what ways does the Holy Spirit provide everything necessary for the church to fulfill God's purposes in the world?

5. Why do the leaders and systems of the world reject and persecute the church?

6. What did Jesus mean when he said his followers are to be salt and light in our world?

7. How is it possible for Christian believers to fall into disunity with one another?

8. What must believers do to maintain unity among themselves?

9. How do members of the church give their lives for the mission of Christ?

10. What is an example of church members opposing structures of injustice and oppression?

11. What is an example of church members working to minimize poverty, ignorance, disease, or suffering?

12. In what ways is the church an extended family to all who participate?

13. In what ways is choosing to participate in the church an extreme decision?

14. In what practical ways do we engage in God's mission to the citizens of the world?

15. What is an example of bearing witness to the kingdom of God?

16. How is God transforming the world through the work of the church?

17. Why does God ask believers to consecrate back to him the good gifts and abilities he has given them?

18. What has been your personal experience of participating in the life of the church?

19. How has your understanding of the church developed over time?

20. What more could you do to involve yourself more fully in God's mission to the world?

A SYMBOLIC COMMITMENT, A MEANS OF GRACE

by Donghwan (Bill) Kwon

Donghwan (Bill) Kwon is a Korean missionary and the chancellor of Southeast Asia Nazarene Bible College as well as the country coordinator and district superintendent for Myanmar.

XII. Baptism

12. We believe that Christian baptism, commanded by our Lord, is a sacrament signifying acceptance of the benefits of the atonement of Jesus Christ, to be administered to believers and declarative of their faith in Jesus Christ as their Savior, and full purpose of obedience in holiness and righteousness.

Baptism being a symbol of the new covenant, young children may be baptized, upon request of parents or guardians who shall give assurance for them of necessary Christian training.

Baptism may be administered by sprinkling, pouring, or immersion, according to the choice of the applicant.

(Matthew 3:1–7; 28:16–20; Acts 2:37–41; 8:35–39; 10:44–48; 16:29–34; 19:1–6; Romans 6:3–4; Galatians 3:26–28; Colossians 2:12; 1 Peter 3:18–22)

In the Philippine churches, the baptismal ceremony is often intertwined with annual church outings. In this part of the region, Christians still prefer full immersion ceremonies, but the majority of the churches do not have baptismal fonts. So they often go to swimming pools for a special baptismal ceremony, which often happens on Sundays, when participants can be baptized following poolside worship. Members bring potluck food to share with each other. As a Korean missionary, I found this baptismal Sunday service at the swimming pool interesting. Indeed, it may be a Philippine version of Acts 2:42–47, where believers worship, fellowship, break bread, and pray together.

The Lord Called Billy

It was the first baptismal Sunday of River of Life Christian Fellowship, which was planted in one of the slum communities called *Rowenas* in the Philippines. When preparing baptismal classes, we were amazed to have fifty-eight candidates in the first year. That day, it took almost two hours to baptize them. Candidates prayerfully waiting along the side of the pool. As they entered the pool, we made sure they had an assurance of salvation through Christ. When the candidate responded affirmatively, we immersed each one for a moment. Then the church community applauded loudly until the next candidate was called.

With fifty-eight candidates waiting in line, it actually turned out to be fifty-nine baptized. A young man named Billy arrived poolside right after the supposedly last candidate, the fifty-eighth, was immersed. Billy assumed it was just a swimming outing with young people in the church. As he appeared, Jackson Natividad, their local pastor, invited him to be baptized. After a moment of slight hesitation, Billy agreed to be baptized. In the few seconds as he was baptized, the Holy Spirit powerfully touched Billy. When he came out of the water, he couldn't stop weeping and trembling. I embraced him and prayed for him as I sensed the strong work of the Spirit in his heart. He later shared his testimony:

As I was walking toward the pastor, I don't know why, but tears started to fall. I had a flashback of what I had been doing. I was immersed in the water, and when I got out of the water, my tears fell again. After that, I felt very light. I felt that someone was embracing me. I talked to the Lord: "Lord, you've shown me what kind of person I am. Is that who I am supposed to be?" After experiencing the power of the Lord, I noticed that I have started avoiding my vices. My routine has changed. I now spend more time in church. My desire is that God continues to transform me. I also pray that he will use me mightily for his kingdom.

The apostle Peter, in Acts 10, witnessed similar experiences. After an unusual dream, Peter was invited by Cornelius, the Roman centurion, to visit the centurion's home. Without understanding all that was unfolding, he followed the Holy Spirit's guidance. Peter experienced the strong work of the Holy Spirit as he preached. This was unimaginable work in the eyes of a Jewish apostle—to be among the Gentiles. As Peter shared, "Surely no one can stand in the way of their being baptized with water. [Gentiles] have received the Holy Spirit just as we have" (v 47).

The Work of the Holy Spirit

Through Billy, I learned that baptism has two essential natures. Believers' baptism is done by the genuine work of the Holy Spirit, and the evidence—the fruit of baptism—is the transformed life of a believer. The baptismal ceremony itself may be a form of ritual that testifies to their salvation. Yet it is the Holy Spirit who penetrates and transforms believers to commit their lives as true disciples to follow Christ. When the Spirit touched Billy, his life was radically changed. Everyone in the community could testify that he became a new being. As a woman of prayer, Billy's mom was also overjoyed at Billy's baptism and his genuine transformation.

Today, Billy is still going house to house in their small community of *Rowenas*, sharing the good news. Now he leads a small discipleship group comprised of young men and women in the community. He is also actively engaged in outreach ministry to a neighboring community. I know Billy's life will not always be free of trouble, but I am sure that the Holy Spirit, who has filled him, will continue to embrace and guide him.

Different Methods, Same Spirit

In the global church, I see different methods for baptismal ceremonies, but the essence of a believer's baptism can only be found when the Holy Spirit is at work. It is still beyond our understanding how the Holy Spirit enters seeking hearts, but it is evident in the lives of believers, as seen with Billy. In our mission field, we are delighted to hear about and witness so many people coming to faith in Jesus Christ and being baptized each year.

Some parents choose to bring their infants to be baptized, seeking the anointment of the Holy Spirit as they commit to raise their children in a godly way. The Church of the Nazarene has always recognized infant baptism as a symbol of parents' or guardians' intentions to raise their children in God's church and their hope to see their children choose God's way when they are older. As the *Manual* states, "Christian baptism signifies for [young children] God's acceptance within the community of Christian faith on the basis of prevenient grace. It anticipates his or her personal confession of faith in Jesus Christ."

We are delighted to recognize and proclaim baptism not as a single event but as a symbolic commitment that invites the Holy Spirit to work visibly and continually in the daily lives of all believers.

Questions for Reflection or Discussion

Think about the material you have read in chapter 12 and consider your responses to the following questions. Use scriptural references to strengthen your answers whenever possible.

1. What is your understanding of the significance of Christian baptism?

2. What questions have you had about Christian baptism?

3. Many Christian traditions, including the Church of the Nazarene, recognize baptism as a sacrament. What does that mean to you?

4. What do we mean when we talk about baptism as a "means of grace"?

5. Why do some believers have an emotional response to their baptism, as Billy related in this chapter?

6. Even though believers decide to present themselves as candidates for baptism, the true meaning of baptism is the work of the Holy Spirit. How is this the case?

7. How do you explain God's transformation of believers' lives after conversion and baptism?

8. How would you describe the continuing work of the Holy Spirit in believers' lives following baptism?

9. Why is the fruit of a transformed life expected of believers?

10. Why does the Church of the Nazarene not specify a specific mode of baptism?

11. Do you believe one mode of baptism is more effective than another? Why or why not?

12. What is the meaning of baptism for infants or small children as recognized by the Church of the Nazarene and other Christian faith groups?

13. What responsibility do parents, guardians, or caregivers assume in presenting an infant or small child for baptism?

14. What responsibility does the local community of faith assume when an infant or small child is baptized?

15. How does infant baptism differ from infant dedication?

16. How is it the case that baptism is not a single event, as articulated by the author of this chapter?

17. Why do you suppose some Christian believers do not present themselves for baptism?

18. How would you go about challenging a non-baptized believer to consider this means of grace?

13 COME TO THE TABLE
by Anna Muller

*Anna Muller (not her real name) is a Nazarene missionary and scholar.
Her name has been changed for security reasons.*

XIII. The Lord's Supper

**13. We believe that the Memorial and Communion Supper
instituted by our Lord and Savior Jesus Christ is essentially a New
Testament sacrament, declarative of his sacrificial death, through
the merits of which believers have life and salvation and promise
of all spiritual blessings in Christ. It is distinctively for those who
are prepared for reverent appreciation of its significance, and by
it they show forth the Lord's death 'til he come again. It being the
Communion feast, only those who have faith in Christ and love for
the saints should be called to participate therein.**

*(Exodus 12:1–14; Matthew 26:26–29; Mark 14:22–25; Luke 22:17–20; John 6:28–58; I
Corinthians 10:14–21; 11:23–32)*

As a small child, I remember my extended family gathered around a
table celebrating the Lunar New Year's Eve. That was one of the most
important celebrations of our culture. It brought us so much joy and
fun. We felt a great sense of hope for the new year. On that evening,
everyone who was at that table was treated like a family member; it did
not matter how long we had known each other.

Dining with the Creator

The image of the table is a warm one in many countries and cultures
around the world. Being at the same table and sharing a meal carries so
much meaning and significance in both relational and social identities.

Can we imagine being at the Lord's Table at "the wedding supper of the Lamb" (Revelation 19:9)—eating and drinking with him, the Creator of the universe?! We will enjoy the exciting and warm fellowship with all the saints from everywhere and through every age. More importantly, we will experience our identity as extremely honored guests of our Lord Jesus. These thoughts encourage us as we anticipate the coming of that day.

Jesus spoke of this great wedding banquet in his earthly ministry (Matthew 26:29), but he also prepared a table for us to fellowship and to experience his presence while we are still on earth. We call it the Lord's Supper. Near the end of his earthly mission, before his crucifixion and resurrection, Jesus gathered his disciples for the Passover meal. He instituted the Lord's Supper on that night, as told in Luke 22:14–20:

When the hour came, Jesus and his apostles reclined at the table. And he said to them, "I have eagerly desired to eat this Passover with you before I suffer. For I tell you, I will not eat it again until it finds fulfillment in the kingdom of God."

After taking the cup, he gave thanks and said, "Take this and divide it among you. For I tell you I will not drink again from the fruit of the vine until the kingdom of God comes."

And he took bread, gave thanks and broke it, and gave it to them, saying, "This is my body given for you; do this in remembrance of me."

In the same way, after the supper he took the cup, saying, "This cup is the new covenant in my blood, which is poured out for you."

Connecting Two Meals

This sacrament has many different names. The most common are the Lord's Supper, Communion, the Eucharist, the Table of the Lord, and the breaking of bread. In the early church, the Lord's Supper and agape love feast were held as one. As time passed, the Lord's Supper separated from the love feast, and eventually became less and less an actual meal. This sacrament connects with two events: the Passover meal Jesus had with his disciples and the future wedding supper of the Lamb.

The Lord's Table is an instituted means of grace, a blessed way of pouring out God's mercy and grace upon his people. Rob Staples wrote in *Outward Sign and Inward Grace* that, if we call baptism the "sacrament of initiation," then the Lord's Supper should be called the "sacrament of sanctification." It is a means of grace for promoting holiness.

Experiencing His Presence

We experience Christ's presence in the Lord's Supper. This presence is not in his humanity but in his divinity, a spiritual presence instead of a bodily one. The objective presence of Christ in the Supper is that of a living and acting person working through the elements. We call it real because it is a "living presence."[1]

Thomas Oden said, "The Lord's Supper is a mode of confession. By partaking of the Lord's Supper, we confess his living presence and lordship. By these appointed means, the church is called regularly to confess Christ until the final reckoning."[2]

Every year, as I anticipated the New Year's Eve supper, the joy and hope in that process got more and more intense as the time drew closer. When I come to the Lord's Supper, I am reminded that the Lord is always with us, and it is getting closer and closer for me to participate in that great banquet with him at the end of time. Not only is the Lord's Supper filled with the solemn beauty of Christ our Lamb and what he has done for us, but it also includes the warmth of fellowship in the family of God and what it means to be called children of God. This table overflows with God's grace. It reminds us that, even before we knew Jesus and his salvation, his Holy Spirit was working in our lives. He is reaching out to every human being in this world through his immeasurable grace. Without the Lamb's sacrifice, none of us can be saved. Sin separated us from God. We cannot save ourselves from this bondage.

1. Rob L. Staples, *Outward Sign and Inward Grace: The Place of Sacraments in Wesleyan Spirituality* (Kansas City, MO: Beacon Hill Press of Kansas City, 1991), 227.

2. Thomas C. Oden, *Life in the Spirit: Systematic Theology: Volume 3* (San Francisco: HarperCollins, 1992), 107.

Thanksgiving Overflows

Salvation comes only through faith in the Son of God—"the Lamb who was slain from the creation of the world" (Revelation 13:8). This grace is so amazing and indescribable that our hearts should burst out in thanksgiving to our heavenly Father for giving us his one and only Son. This is why we say grace overflows from this Table; thanksgiving overflows to our God for his grace.

The Table also reminds us of God's love. Jesus said, "This is my body given for you," and "my blood, which is poured out for you" (Luke 22:19, 20). Christ died for us even when we were sinners. Until we get older and become more self-aware, we do not fully understand what sin is and how weak and fragile we are in the face of temptation. Only as we mature and grow in our faith can we fully understand how amazing and precious God's redemptive grace is in our lives. He sacrificed his one and only Son so that we can be called his children and inherit the blessings and hopes that come from him. When we tear a piece of bread from the loaf, it reminds us of the One who was torn so we can be reconciled with our God. When we pour the juice, it whispers to us of the One who poured out his lifeblood so we can be forgiven and live forever. Jesus said, "So the one who feeds on me will live because of me" (John 6:57b). "Do this in remembrance of me" (Luke 22:19c). If we truly love Jesus, we will obey his command. We remember him not just from memory but from a much deeper and intimate recollection of every encounter with him, which brings that first love once again to our hearts. That is the "remembrance" that Jesus encouraged.

Ultimate Hope

This Table gives ultimate hope for all believers. We were created by Jesus and for him. He never intended for us to live separated from the Life Giver. When we gather around the table, we realize who we truly are and why we are here on earth. We neither belong to ourselves nor to the world; we are "a royal priesthood, a holy nation" (1 Peter 2:9). This identity brings a greater hope.

Sometimes we lose our focus and get caught up in the concerns of this world. Remember, we are preparing ourselves for the wedding supper of the Lamb. The hope of being at rest with Jesus forever offers light in the dark night. It also recalls his promise that he will come again to bring us home. "I tell you, I will not drink from this fruit of the vine from now on until that day when I drink it new with you in my Father's kingdom" (Matthew 26:29).

All Believers Bound Together

This Table also binds all believers together in the love of Christ. Jesus commanded his disciples on the night he instituted the Lord's Supper to love one another just as he had loved them. The Creator of the universe humbled himself to wash his creatures' feet so they could learn what it means to love one another. When we come to the Table, we remember that we were sinners; none is better than any other. None deserve God's grace. Therefore, none should look down on another for any reason. We should ask the Lord to continually give us heaven's perspective so we can love unconditionally, like our Lord Jesus. As human beings, we are not perfect in deed, but we can be made perfect in Christ's love. Jesus reminded us that when we love one another, the world recognizes us as his disciples. This Table erases boundary lines separating gender, age, culture, language, social status, and everything the world uses to divide people into broken segments. The Lord's Supper erases lines and unites all believers together as one before him.

The Lord's Supper is similar to that big, warm, and hopeful New Year's Eve meal of my childhood, but at the same time, the Eucharist is much more meaningful. We long to be with Christ; he longs to be with us. Whether you imagine a wedding banquet or a family celebration, Christ's presence is the most important thing, and that is everything.

Come, let us join with one accord
Who share the supper of the Lord,
Our Lord and Master's praise to sing;
Nourished on earth with living bread,
We now are at his table fed,
But wait to see our heavenly King;
To see the great Invisible
Without a sacramental veil,

With all his robes of glory on,
In rapturous joy and love and praise
Him to behold with open face,
High on his everlasting throne.
(Charles Wesley)

Questions for Reflection or Discussion

Think about the material you have read in chapter 13 and consider your responses to the following questions. Use scriptural references to strengthen your answers whenever possible.

1. Recount some of your favorite memories of family meals shared together.

2. What are some of your favorite elements of participating in the Lord's Supper?

3. In what ways does connecting the Lord's Supper with the wedding supper of the Lamb (Revelation 19:9) add meaning and anticipation to participating in the Lord's Supper?

4. What do we mean when we say we experience the presence of the Lord Jesus when we participate in the Lord's Supper?

5. In what ways is the Lord's Supper a means of God's grace?

6. What features of God's grace come into clear focus in the Lord's Supper?

7. How does the Lord's Supper promote holiness?

8. In what ways do we confess Christ when we participate in the Lord's Supper?

9. Explain how the Lord's Supper can be a uniting moment for the children of God.

10. The act of breaking bread calls to remembrance the broken body of Christ. What spiritual significance may be understood from Christ's body being broken for you?

11. The drinking of juice calls to remembrance the spilled blood of Christ. What spiritual significance may be understood from Christ's blood being spilled for you?

12. In what ways do we remember Christ in the Lord's Supper?

13. In what ways does the Lord's Supper strengthen our hope?

14. Why do you think Jesus said, "I will not drink of this fruit of the vine from now on until that day when I drink it new with you in my Father's kingdom" (Matthew 26:29)?

15. Think of a time in your life when you suspended participation in an activity or consumption of a food or beverage until an anticipated event came to reality. How did this exercise heighten your anticipation and hope?

16. Why did Jesus connect the Lord's Supper with love for one another?

17. How does the Lord's Supper help us focus on heaven's perspective?

18. How are Christians made perfect in Christ's love?

19. Describe how participation in the Lord's Supper helps erase boundary lines between believers.

20. How can faith be strengthened by realizing that Christ is as eager to be with us at the wedding banquet of the Lamb as we are to be with him?

14 A GOD WHO HEALS
by Erika Rocha

Erika Rocha and her husband, Marco, are pastors of the Villa Lugano Church of the Nazarene in Buenos Aires, Argentina.

XIV. Divine Healing

14. We believe in the Bible doctrine of divine healing and urge our people to offer the prayer of faith for the healing of the sick. We also believe God heals through the means of medical science.

(2 Kings 5:1–19; Psalm 103:1–5; Matthew 4:23–24; 9:18–35; John 4:46–54; Acts 5:12–16; 9:32–42; 14:8–15; 1 Corinthians 12:4–11; 2 Corinthians 12:7–10; James 5:13–16)

We believe in a God who heals. We believe in faith-filled prayer for the healing of the sick. We preach this with joy, teach it to the next generation, and practice it every time we have the chance.

I grew up in the Church of the Nazarene. That is where I was shaped as a woman and follower of Jesus Christ. I met my husband in the church; we formed a family, and today we minister as the pastors of a thriving congregation in the southern part of the city of Buenos Aires, Argentina. Many testimonies come to mind of healing that God has done—some of them so glorious that they gave way to a spiritual awakening in the congregations where they occurred. Nonetheless, I can also remember the times when God did not heal, or when healing did not come in the way we expected.

Joy, Then Heartache

I was finishing my formation in seminary alongside my husband, and we were ready to begin our first pastorate in a small congregation on the outskirts of Buenos Aires. The church eagerly awaited us, and we, along with our three-year-old girl and a baby on the way, were happy to begin serving the Lord there. Everything was ready for our family and our congregation to enjoy this new season in our lives. Our son was born on the expected date, and we experienced the blessing of life once more. But this moment of joy would also bring moments we will never forget.

Soon after he was born, our son presented respiratory problems and had to go to an intensive-care unit. Our newborn's life was at stake, and the prognosis was uncertain. My husband and I faced the moment with the same faith that sustained us during so many difficult moments in our lives. We trusted once again in our God, and we prayed for our child to be healed. The church, friends, family, and even people we did not know joined us in prayer for healing as we waited on God. But the days went by, and I could not concentrate on my postpartum recuperation. I lost my appetite and only thought about crying out to the Lord for the life of my son. Not being able to have him by my side broke my heart. Every time we were allowed to see him, all I could do was hold his tiny hand and pray.

Four days after his birth, the doctors informed us that our son's situation had worsened and that there was nothing else they could do. We were asked to say goodbye to our precious son. My husband and I entered the intensive-care unit one last time, we got close to our child, held him in our arms, and, with tears in our eyes and a mixed sensation of pain and hope, we prayed one last time. We left the unit, and just a few minutes later, the doctors informed us that our little boy had gone to be with the Lord.

Heartache, Then Healing

This experience marked my life and that of my family. After going through this painful situation, we understood more profoundly that God heals in many ways, and not just physically. The pain of imagining our boy accompanying us in ministry—and now knowing he never would—pushed us toward having an encounter with another aspect of our healing God. God healed our hearts. God restored our family. God demonstrated love to us through the brothers and sisters who walked alongside us during this entire process. And God helped us experience a supernatural dimension of faith that we may not have gotten from any other situation.

It's easy to reduce divine healing to the physical. Nevertheless, God wants to heal in many ways. Psalm 147:3 shows us the God who heals our emotions: "He heals the brokenhearted and binds up their wounds." We can also affirm that there is no healthier life than the one that walks in holiness, even when the body is ill. The apostle Paul teaches in 2 Corinthians 4:16: "Therefore we do not lose heart. Though outwardly we are wasting away, yet inwardly we are being renewed day by day." Many people throughout their Christian journeys have changed destructive habits to the benefit of their physical, mental, and emotional health. The Lord helps us value that which we did not care for, including our health, as the apostle Paul expresses in 1 Thessalonians 5:23b: "May your whole spirit, soul and body be kept blameless at the coming of our Lord Jesus Christ."

If we consider that our bodies form part of a whole and that God sees us that way, we will be better prepared to comprehend that God heals in many ways, and not always as we expect. In their book *Fully Alive: Discovering the Adventure of Healthy and Holy Living*, Jerry and Larry Hull affirm the following: "We can look around us or at the mirror that stares back at us and find limited, flawed . . . people. The route to comprehensive health begins when we recognize our limitations and accept them as opportunities, challenges, and adventures."

Healing, However God Chooses

When we refer to divine healing, it is important to avoid the temptation to believe that God is at our beck and call to heal us whenever we request it, as if it were God's obligation to do whatever we want. This false concept has wreaked havoc on the church, leading many to follow a God who seems more like a cosmic magician instead of the sovereign God who desires to manifest himself with power over his children in the ways he chooses.

Despite the painful experience of losing our son, my husband and I assumed the commitment to pastor the congregation that awaited us. During the years that we ministered there, God used our precious brothers and sisters as well as other minister friends to heal our wounds. A few years later, the Lord blessed us with the arrival of another son, who today is growing rapidly, and who accompanies us in our ministry efforts alongside his sister. We find that God has placed couples close to us who have been through the pain of losing a baby, to whom we are able to minister and help experience this other aspect of divine healing.

Let us pray with faith, trusting that the response to the pleas for healing God has prepared for us will come when and how God decides because God is sovereign. Let us learn to fully trust and rest in our Lord.

Questions for Reflection or Discussion

Think about the material you have read in chapter 14 and consider your responses to the following questions. Use scriptural references to strengthen your answers whenever possible.

1. What has been your understanding of divine healing prior to reading this chapter?

2. What common misconceptions of divine healing persist in your cultural setting?

3. How do you believe God answers prayers for healing?

4. Do you believe a lack of divine healing results from a lack of faith?

5. How does God sometimes heal in ways other than physical healing?

6. In what ways does God support and sustain believers in times when he does not answer with divine healing?

7. In what ways do members of the community of faith support and sustain believers in times when God does not answer with divine healing?

8. How might God bring about healing other than by miraculous means?

9. According to Article of Faith XIV, what is the position of the Church of the Nazarene regarding consulting physicians and taking medicine?

10. What responsibility do we have to eat right, exercise, and participate in practices that promote good health?

11. What are some principles to keep in mind in coming to terms with infirmities, chronic pain, or illnesses from which God does not deliver us?

12. How might believers who continue to live with infirmities, chronic pain, or illnesses be wounded healers who are uniquely able to minister to others with similar issues?

13. How is it possible to have faith in our own faith for healing rather than faith in God?

14. What are the dangers of having faith in our own faith?

15. What elements should characterize our prayers of faith for divine healing?

16. How can we best learn to trust and rest in Christ regardless of whether he answers prayers for healing as we request?

15 CHRIST IS COMING AGAIN*

by Jon Twitchell

Jon Twitchell currently serves the Nazarene Foundation as a vice president of gift planning.

XV. Second Coming of Christ

15. We believe that the Lord Jesus Christ will come again; that we who are alive at his coming shall not precede them that are asleep in Christ Jesus; but that, if we are abiding in him, we shall be caught up with the risen saints to meet the Lord in the air, so that we shall ever be with the Lord.

(Matthew 25:31–46; John 14:1–3; Acts 1:9–11; Philippians 3:20–21; 1 Thessalonians 4:13–18; Titus 2:11–14; Hebrews 9:26–28; 2 Peter 3:3–15; Revelation 1:7–8; 22:7–20)

The first fourteen Church of the Nazarene Articles of Faith proclaim what Scripture has revealed about who God is, what God has done, and what God is doing. The fifteenth Article turns our attention toward the future. The doctrine of the second coming looks toward the return of Christ and our final redemption at the end of the world. With this shift in focus comes recognition that we tread on much more fragile territory. Instead of retelling the story of what has already happened and explaining how it impacts us today, we are now faced with the task of attempting to understand how God brings this grand narrative of redemption into its great and glorious conclusion.

---

*Excerpted from a 2004 sermon delivered at the Cape Elizabeth Church of the Nazarene in Maine.

As we study prophecy, we must be guided by the principle that Scripture should never be interpreted to mean something drastically different from what it meant to its original audience. Any interpretation should not only make sense to us but should also have made sense to the original hearers. If the prophecy had not made sense to them in their time, they would not have been likely to preserve and pass it down from generation to generation.

Eschatology

The study of end times is called *eschatology*. The language of eschatology is robust and complicated, with numerous phrases and words used to describe different camps of belief. The large camps of belief are categorized into pre-millennialism, post-millennialism, and a-millennialism. Within the group of pre-millennialists, we find those who believe in a secret rapture, and those believers are often further categorized as pre-, mid-, and post-tribulationists. Instead of attempting to define each of those positions, let's consider some of the questions that divide these camps:

Will there be a literal, thousand-year reign of Christ on the earth (a millennial kingdom)? Will this millennial reign be brought about by Christ's return? Or will Christ reign through the church at work throughout the world, bringing about the kingdom of God in reality for one thousand years prior to the physical return of Christ?

Did the events in Revelation partly occur in AD 70 with the fall of the temple and of Jerusalem? Or have none of the events in the book of Revelation yet occurred?

When Jesus returns, will he be escorted to earth by the believers to set up his kingdom, or will he rapture them to heaven while a tribulation is meted upon the wicked? If there is a tribulation of the unsaved, will Jesus steal his bride away before, during, or after?

Is the tribulation something endured by nonbelievers? Or is it a great tribulation of the saints?

Is it possible to know any dates? Or even to recognize the signs of the times?

Different Conclusions

These questions are studied and debated by laypeople, pastors, and theologians all over the world. Scholars and theologians who have studied for years arrive at different conclusions. Pastors attempt to interpret those conclusions and provide them to laypeople who are also surrounded with all sorts of popular theology and literature on the topic—much of which is not consistent with a Wesleyan approach to scriptural interpretation.

Sometimes people are surprised to learn that the Church of the Nazarene doesn't require members to belong to a particular eschatological camp. Instead, our fifteenth Article of Faith focuses on the core essentials. As important as it is to notice what our Article of Faith *does* say, it is also important to notice what it doesn't mention at all. For example, notice that there is no specific mention of a secret rapture of the church.

Some might ask, "Isn't 'caught up . . . to meet the Lord in the air' the same as a secret rapture?" Not necessarily. Just because there is a meeting in the air, the Article does not state where Jesus and the saints go *after* the meeting. Scholars have pointed out that the word for *meet* used in 1 Thessalonians 4 is the same word that is used to describe a welcoming committee that goes out to meet a visiting dignitary and escort him back into town. In that case, it might not be that the saints are raptured away but, rather, that the saints go to meet the Lord in the air, welcoming him back to earth to establish his kingdom. Our Article of Faith doesn't take a position on this one way or another. We also don't take an official position about what is meant by "the great tribulation," or about the millennial kingdom. Much is left unsaid in our Article of Faith—leaving freedom for study and a multitude of opinions.

It may be tempting to wish for a single, authorized view on eschatology. However, it is helpful to remember that there are countless scholars throughout the centuries who have come to far different conclusions about these matters. Does this mean we should stop caring? Does it mean we should ignore any discussion of end times and the return of Christ? I don't think so. We should absolutely study Scripture.

No harm exists in exploring the different theories about how this age might come to a conclusion. But let's remember that, for the most part, these are untestable theories that should not rise to the level of dogma. We should be careful of being so focused on various eschatological theories that we stop focusing on how to live our lives today.

Christ Will Come Again

At the same time, we recognize that, while there is disagreement among scholars and theologians, we can come to solid agreement on the things that are stated in our Article of Faith—namely that Christ will return, the dead will be raised, the risen and living saints will be caught up to meet him in the air, and that we will always be with the Lord. These are the solid points of faith in the second advent of Christ that are nonnegotiable.

Much of the wording for our Article of Faith is drawn from Paul's letters to the believers in Thessalonica. Believing that Christ would return in their lifetime, these saints were concerned about those who had already died before the second coming. In the midst of their grief and doubt, Paul offered them the assurance of Christ's return and the hope of resurrection for all who died in Christ.

"Encourage one another with these words" (I Thessalonians 4:18): *Christ will come again.*

Are the skies cloudy and gray? Christ will come again.

Does the load seem too heavy to bear? Christ will come again.

Are you grieving? Christ will come again.

Are you sick? Christ will come again.

Are you in distress? Christ will come again.

Are you discouraged by evil's influence in the world? Christ will come again.

When it seems like darkness and death are winning, when it seems like the forces of evil are too strong, when the clouds are covering the sky: look to the east, for Christ will come again.

A Solid Rock of Hopeful Optimism

Put in that context, our Article of Faith is not wishy-washy at all but, rather, a solid rock of hopeful optimism that allows us to look toward the future, even in uncertain times. Some might wish that our church had taken a position on pre-, post-, or a-millennialism or pre-, mid-, or post-tribulationalism. We might want an official, dogmatic position on the end times so that when someone asks, "What do Nazarenes believe about the rapture?" we can answer them. Instead, by not taking a decisive stand on divisive doctrinal issues, we have done more to focus on the main thing: *Christ will come again.*

After all, how will we know who is right about the millennial kingdom? At the end of the age, after it all happens. How will we know who is right about raptures and tribulations? At the end of the age, after it all happens. Consider this: At the end of the age, after it all happens, we won't be sitting around in a room discussing who was right and who was wrong. No pins, keychains, or necklaces will be given to those who figured out all the details. Instead, we will be united together with Christ Jesus for eternity.

The far more important questions are these: How do we live in the meantime? How does our belief in Christ's return affect how we live today? Our call is to live faithfully in the right here and the right now. Informed by the hopeful certainty that Christ will come again, our tasks are the same as they have always been: to love God and neighbor, to proclaim good tidings of great joy, to care for God's creation, to welcome the stranger, to provide for the orphan and widow, and to faithfully live out God's mission in our present-day lives.

Questions for Reflection or Discussion

Think about the material you have read in chapter 15 and consider your responses to the following questions. Use scriptural references to strengthen your answers whenever possible.

1. What is your earliest memory of thinking about the second coming of Christ?

2. Why has interest increased in theories about the second coming in the last 150 years?

3. What popular views about the second coming of Christ have you heard?

4. How has your understanding of the second coming of Christ matured over time?

5. What is the difference between the dozens of theories offered concerning the second coming of Christ and the clear teachings of Scripture, such as forgiveness of sins and the lordship of Jesus Christ?

6. Why is it important not to allow the many theories about the second coming to occupy a central place in our witness to the world about Jesus Christ?

7. Why do you think the Church of the Nazarene does not take a particular view on second-coming theories?

8. Would you rather the Church of the Nazarene affirm clear statements of Scripture, as it does in Article XV, or would you prefer that it speculate on the numerous possibilities of how Christ might return?

9. Why do you think the Church of the Nazarene does not offer a specific teaching on such theories as the secret rapture, great tribulation, or millennial kingdom?

10. What does the author of the chapter mean when he says, "these are untestable theories that should not rise to the level of dogma"?

11. Looking at Article XV, what clear statements can we affirm from Scripture about the second coming of Christ?

12. Read 1 Thessalonians 4:13–18 and name the ideas found in this passage that are echoed in Article XV.

13. What encouragement do you find in the biblical affirmation "Christ will come again?"

14. Looking beyond all of the second-coming theories offered this side of eternity, what do you think will be the central focus of your attention once you reach heaven?

15. With eager anticipation of the second coming of Christ, how should we live in the meantime?

16. More specifically, name some action steps you can take today to live confidently and hopefully in Christ as you await his return.

16 THIS IS OUR HOPE

by Ruth I. Cordova

Ruth I. Cordova is a missionary in Guatemala, serving as a professor of theology, Bible, and pastoral courses at the Nazarene Seminary.

XVI. Resurrection, Judgment, and Destiny

16. We believe in the resurrection of the dead, that the bodies both of the just and the unjust shall be raised to life and united with their spirits—"they that have done good, unto the resurrection of life; and they that have done evil, unto the resurrection of damnation."

16.1. We believe in future judgment in which every person shall appear before God to be judged according to his or her deeds in life.

16.2. We believe that glorious and everlasting life is assured to all who savingly believe in, and obediently follow, Jesus Christ our Lord; and that the finally impenitent shall suffer eternally in hell.

(Genesis 18:25; 1 Samuel 2:10; Psalm 50:6; Isaiah 26:19; Daniel 12:2–3; Matthew 25:31–46; Mark 9:43–48; Luke 16:19–31; 20:27–38; John 3:16–18; 5:25–29; 11:21–27; Acts 17:30–31; Romans 2:1–16; 14:7–12; 1 Corinthians 15:12–58; 2 Corinthians 5:10; 2 Thessalonians 1:5–10; Revelation 20:11–15; 22:1–15)

This Article of Faith is an important one, but in some ways it is difficult to respond to all the questions we may have about the final resurrection, judgment, and destiny of humankind. As human beings, we would like to know all the details about life after death and our final destiny. As Christians, we would like to find the information and explanation of these matters in Scripture and fully understand the reasons for our beliefs.

When we read in the Bible the stories of some of the Old Testament prophets like Elisha, who in God's power restored people to life, or the story of Jesus in the New Testament, when he raised Lazarus and others from the dead, maybe we felt goose bumps or got excited to know that the person who was dead was brought back to life. We identify with the characters and situations of those accounts. We feel sad and hopeless for the loss of life.

But as we continue reading, we are surprised by the faith of people in these stories who do not give up hope in the midst of the pain but run to look for God's prophet or to ask Jesus to do something about it. Then, emotions change. Faith, hope, and expectation exist. These stories now have a happy ending. What joy! God has raised a loved one from the dead!

Jesus Is Risen

The favorite Bible story all of us like to read or hear about is, of course, the story of Jesus's resurrection. We can identify with the disciples' emotions and feelings after Jesus's death—sadness, pain, hopelessness, fear, worries, and doubts. Then, as the story continues, we identify with the women who get up early on the first day of the week to go to Jesus's tomb, just to discover that he is not there. They are surprised by an angel who tells them that Jesus has risen from the dead just like he had said he would. We experience great joy in our hearts at this turn of events. Yes! Jesus is risen!

Jesus has defeated death by returning to life. Jesus has a body and is not a ghost. Jesus looks as he did before he died—but radiant in glory. Jesus speaks, feels, and even eats with his disciples. And, finally, God will raise us too, just as God raised Jesus. *This is our hope.* This is why the resurrection of Jesus Christ is an important event in human history and for the Christian faith.

Perhaps we don't feel the excitement of an immediate resurrection when someone very dear to us dies. Instead, we ask ourselves questions such as, *Why did she die? Did he experience pain, fear, or suffering in the moment of death? Is she living in peace, or is she being punished for wrongdoing? Where is his spirit? What is she doing?* These are questions about life after death, judgment, heaven, and hell. We ask these questions because we all want to know, in some way, what is going to happen to us when we die.

Resurrection of the Body

Our sixteenth Article of Faith came from Methodism and the Anglican Church, although the Church of the Nazarene elaborated on it a little more. Belief in the resurrection of the body is part of the Christian faith (church creeds and traditions) and is important because of the resurrection of Jesus Christ in the history of humankind. When reading Scripture, we find stories and teachings about the immortality of the soul and the resurrection (Job 19:25–26; Psalm 49:15; 90:10; Ecclesiastes 3:21; Isaiah 26:19; Daniel 12:2; Matthew 10:28; 17:3; 22:31–32; Luke 12:4–5; 16:22–23; 20:34–36; 23:43, 46; John 5:26, 28–29; 11:25–26; Acts 7:59; 24:15; Philippians 3:21; 2 Timothy 1:10). Thus, all Jews believed in the resurrection except the Sadducees, who denied any resurrection of the dead and any afterlife, and held that the soul perished at death, therefore denying any penalty or reward after the earthly life.

In the Bible, we find pieces of information here and there about the last things told by different people in different occasions, situations, and contexts at different times in the history of humankind, using both concrete and metaphorical language. Sometimes this information is given as answers to questions or as explanations of certain truths; at other times, it is given as a way to prepare the disciples for persecution in the future and to encourage new Christians to persevere.

For instance, Paul wrote in his first letter to the Thessalonians about the coming of the Lord and stated two important truths in 4:13–14: First, Christians are not to grieve as others who do not have hope. Second, Christians believe that Jesus died and rose again and that, therefore, God will raise the dead too. This makes a big difference in the way we understand death.

A New Body

What is going to happen with the body after a person dies? Some Christians think the body needs to be preserved for the day of resurrection. They show concern if someone dies by being burned, eaten by an animal, lost at sea, or if the body is cremated. They ask, "How will this person be raised at the resurrection if he or she doesn't have a body?" We know from Scripture, however, that the earthly body dies and becomes dust. The Word says, "For dust you are and to dust you will return" (Genesis 3:19). It doesn't matter what happens to the human body, or "natural body," as Paul calls it. This body is not going to enter the other side because, as the apostle also says, it is a "perishable body" (I Corinthians 15:42–44, 50).

Also according to these and other scriptures, God will give us a new body at the resurrection, a heavenly body. Paul explains that this new body is a spiritual body (I Corinthians 15:44) and that this mortal body must put on immortality (I Corinthians 15:53). It is a new creation (2 Corinthians 5:17). In the resurrection, transformed bodies will be raised to life and united to their spirits (Philippians 3:21; I John 3:2). Resurrected bodies will be free from illness, pain, suffering, and death. They will be glorious bodies like Jesus's.

We do not know for sure when the dead will receive their new bodies. There are passages in Paul's writings that indicate that it could be as soon as they die (2 Corinthians 5:1–7; Philippians 1:21–24), or perhaps not until the final resurrection (I Corinthians 15:23; Philippians 3:20–21). The resurrection of the dead in the final day means that everyone will be raised, whether just or unjust, and will be judged according to faith in Christ, actions, thoughts, words, intentions, emotions, and beliefs, as well as what was left undone in their lives. Judgment will be both revelatory and thorough.

Final Judgment

What will the judgment look like? Revelation 20:11–15 describes the judgment itself. Jesus Christ will be the judge because he knows the hearts of all people. He understands their actions, their deeper thoughts and motives. He is the Son of God and he *is* God. But Jesus Christ is also the Son of Man, who became like humans (Philippians 2:6–7), and after he died, God exalted him and gave him the authority to judge both the living and the dead (Acts 17:31; 10:42). The time of the judgment of humankind is known as the Day of the Lord (Acts 17:31; Romans 2:5, 16; 2 Peter 2:9; Jude 6; Revelation 6:17). No one knows when it will be, how long it will last, or where it will be.

Nazarene theologian H. Orton Wiley suggested there will be certain principles and standards upon which the judgment will be based, as defined by Christ (Luke 12:48; John 12:48), and mentioned by the apostle Paul in his letter to the Romans (2:7–11). The standard by which all will be judged on the last day will be based on the light or truth revealed to them (Romans 2:14–16; Hebrews 10:28–29). The people to be judged will be numerous and difficult to count (Revelation 7:9; 20:12). They will come from all nations and races, speak different languages and dialects, be of all ages and genders, come from different social and economic conditions and different periods of history—but all of them will have descended from Adam and Eve, since the world was created by God.

The good and the evil will have everlasting life but will experience it differently.

Those who believed in Jesus and obeyed him (his Word, walked in the Spirit, faith in actions) will live in communion with Jesus and other believers for eternity. They will experience joy, happiness, and peace and will praise and worship the Lord forever. Scriptures state that heaven will be the place where the just will abide in their final state of glorification. Jesus refers to "my Father's house" (John 14:2–3), and Paul calls it the "third heaven" (2 Corinthians 12:2). It is a place where there is no sin, death, or pain (Revelation 21:4, 27). The just will serve the Lamb (Revelation 22:3–5) and enjoy fellowship one with another and the Lord (Matthew 8:11; Hebrews 12:22–23). The redeemed will express and increase their love and intellectual faculties and will understand God's love, wisdom, and power. Above all, creation will be renewed, and the redeemed will abide in a new heaven and new earth (Revelation 21:2, 9–10).

Those who rejected Jesus and his salvation, walked away from the light, and followed their own hearts will die in their own sin and live separated from God forever (Matthew 25:41; Revelation 20:14–15; 21:8). They will live lonely and sad in the darkness, tormented by hatred, shame, pride, blasphemy, and fear. They will be exposed to the corruption of their own souls (Matthew 8:12; 22:13; 25:30–46).

Walk in Perfect Love

There are several truths and lessons we can learn from this Article of Faith and apply to our lives:

The bodily resurrection of the dead is a truth that tells us that there is life after death. Therefore, all human beings will be raised and continue living forever. This is possible because of Jesus's resurrection.

The judgment is a real truth that no one can escape. At the end of our lives, we will be judged by our Creator. Whether it will be a time of joy or regret will depend on our response to the opportunity given to us to know God and his Word and to live like Jesus and do good on earth while we were alive.

We know that our actions on this earth will count in our final judgment. We need to live every day with an awareness of our obligation to be responsible stewards of the prevenient and salvific grace of God—since every good thing we do as Christians is founded on God's grace and empowered by the Holy Spirit. Let us continually ask ourselves, *Is what I do in my life done in love, holiness, and goodness? Am I modeling Jesus's love? Am I attracting others to God because of my interest in them? Am I using my abilities and resources to advance the kingdom of God? Am I doing what God asks me to do, or do I prefer to be indifferent, negligent, or ignore it?*

We need to walk in perfect love and not be found lacking in such love.

Questions for Reflection or Discussion

Think about the material you have read in chapter 16 and consider your responses to the following questions. Use scriptural references to strengthen your answers whenever possible.

1. What questions come to mind when you think about life after death and eternity?

2. Why have people pondered answers to these questions throughout human history?

3. In what ways does the resurrection of Jesus offer us hope regarding our eternal future?

4. What is the significance of Scripture affirming that Jesus had a body following his resurrection?

5. Why do you think most cultures and religions of the world believe in life after death?

6. In what ways do you think our resurrected bodies will differ from our earthly bodies?

7. Why does the Church of the Nazarene believe that both righteous and unrighteous people will be resurrected for judgment?

8. Who will be the judge in the final judgment?

9. How is this judge uniquely suited to pass judgment on all humanity?

10. How should we prepare for the Day of the Lord?

11. How will people who have never heard the name of Jesus be judged?

12. Why does the Church of the Nazarene believe that the judgment passed on the righteous and unrighteous is final and without appeal?

13. Describe in your own words God's new heaven and new earth.

14. Describe what you believe heaven will be like.

15. Why should no one desire the judgment of hell?

16. Why does sin against God bring such terrible punishment?

17. Having considered the biblical truth of Article XVI, how should we live our daily lives?

18. What do you anticipate most about living for eternity in heaven?

LET THE CONVERSATIONS BEGIN

by Frank Moore

We have spent time together taking a fresh look at the sixteen Articles of Faith of the Church of the Nazarene. We have considered a variety of topics of the Christian faith from God's creation of the world to the new creation at the end of this age. Those discussions have brought up dozens of questions for which we have attempted many answers. Now the time has arrived for us to take the information we have reviewed and the perspectives we have gained into our world. It's time to begin listening with new ears to people's questions—in our families, at work, and with the neighbors. The purpose of taking a fresh look at our Articles of Faith goes beyond gaining new knowledge or understanding for our own good. We need to take what we've learned and join in God's mission of sharing the good news of forgiveness of sins, transformation, and sanctification with our friends, family members, and acquaintances.

Contemporary culture is opening conversations that need our input. The global migration of entire groups of people brings unique cultures, beliefs, and practices right into our neighborhoods, offering the opportunity for new conversations. Technology continually changes the way we interact with one another and with the world at large. We find ourselves talking about the best ways to negotiate this new reality. People all around us are asking a variety of new questions. To be honest with you, I've never imagined some of these conversations, so I don't have a fund of knowledge from which to draw. But I do have the Bible, the Articles of Faith, and the support of brothers and sisters in Christ to assist me with answers.

I learned a ministry principle during my seminary education that challenges me to this day. Our professor told us that effective ministry only happens when we listen carefully to the questions people are asking both within the faith community and in the community at large. Then we have the responsibility to answer those questions from a biblical perspective. People tend to listen to what we have to say when we attempt to answer the questions rolling around in their heads. We've just spent time studying the Articles of Faith of the Church of the Nazarene together, so we have fresh insights to offer.

I've been listening to probing questions just like the ones you may hear or have yourself. Let's explore what provokes people to deeper thought. Then let's go to the Bible, to Christian tradition, to reason enlightened by the Holy Spirit, and to personal experiences for answers.

Bringing contemporary topics into focus from a Christian perspective can be a messy business for a number of reasons.

- These topics are not always safe. Some are delicate; others are downright uncomfortable.
- We often fear these topics because they take us into unfamiliar territory.
- We haven't previously talked enough about some of these issues, so we don't always have clearly formed beliefs.
- We often don't have immediate answers to complex questions because we're still working together for an appropriate response.

These conversations will continue to take place in our culture regardless of whether we join them. We must overcome our fears and engage fully in these discussions, appearing at the table in order to help direct conversations toward biblical truth. We need each other to explore God's Word and allow the Spirit of God to enlighten us in these matters. This reality makes some people uncomfortable; they'd rather stick to discussions that have quick and easy answers. But that's not where most people live. The answers to their questions are neither quick nor easy. Their daily lives are complex and demanding as they work their way through the uncharted waters of contemporary society. That's why we need to move to the cutting edge of relevant issues and invite conversations in our homes, at work, and within our faith communities that allow God's light to shine and bring clearer understanding.

I challenge you to join in this endeavor. Recall the issues and perspectives we have discussed in this book. Think carefully about the ways they apply to real-life situations; then engage in provocative conversations with your friends. We need everyone at the table—older adults, young adults, and youth—contributing unique perspectives. Ask the Lord to help you find ways to bring the light of God's Word into these conversations. God's Spirit faithfully works to penetrate the hearts and minds of people with divine truths. Hebrews 4:12 reminds us, "For the word of God is alive and active. Sharper than any double-edged sword, it penetrates even to dividing soul and spirit, joints and marrow; it judges the thoughts and attitudes of the heart."

Let God use you to offer good news from the Word in your conversations as you fully engage the questions of our ever-changing world. We want men, women, youth, and children to come to a saving and sanctifying experience in Jesus Christ. Then we want to disciple them in their faith until they begin to disciple others. All of our efforts together will help us fulfill our mission to make Christlike disciples in the nations. May God bless your life of ministry and service for the kingdom.